Almost Grown fuses theology with principles of practical Christian life in order to give parents and young people models for working together to meet the challenges of the teenage years. Dr. Oraker tells what to expect at each stage of adolescent development, how to cope, and what parents can specifically do to help. Above all, *Almost Grown* aids the Christian parent in bringing his or her child to a new, more mature, ever developing relationship with Christ. Dr. Oraker proves that teenagers and parents need not be strangers, but can rather be companions on the road to maturity.

James R. Oraker, Ph.D., is a Clinical Psychologist and Counselor. He is Staff Psychologist for Young Life and is the Training Director of the Dale House Project, working with adolescents and their families. Dr. Oraker and his family live in Colorado Springs. *Char Meredith* is a Senior Editor at *Young Life.*

ALMOST GROWN

Almost Grown

A CHRISTIAN GUIDE FOR PARENTS OF TEENAGERS

✦

Dr. JAMES R. ORAKER

with CHAR MEREDITH

1817

Published in San Francisco by Harper & Row, Publishers

NEW YORK | SAN FRANCISCO | HAGERSTOWN | LONDON

FIRST EDITION

Designed by Jim Mennick

Library of Congress Cataloging in Publication Data

Oraker, James R
    ALMOST GROWN.

    1. Adolescence. 2. Children—Management.
3. Family—Religious life. I. Meredith, Char, joint author. II. Title.
HQ772.067 1980   649'.125   78-20585
ISBN 0-06-066393-6

80 81 82 83 84 10 9 8 7 6 5 4 3 2 1

TO: *Judy, my wife and loving companion, and our children:*

Jeffrey Eric, who loves the adventure of life
Jennifer Beth, a delightful touch of sunshine
Jason Christopher Rutledge, a special gift of love

Contents

Acknowledgments

Char Meredith, a friend and professional writer, edited, re-wrote, interviewed, and introduced concepts to make the manuscript readable as well as helpful. Her skills and personal sensitivity to the subject make her contributions to the book most meaningful. Thus, her name appears on the title page.

Vicki Smith spent long hours at the typewriter preparing the manuscript for publication. Her time and dedication to excellence is greatly appreciated. Also thanks to Becky Tomaszewski, who got the earliest sections into typing, and who has worked faithfully alongside to bring the manuscript to its detailed conclusion.

My wife, Judy, has encouraged me to say something about the importance of the Christian family and of adolescence at this particular time in our history. She and our children, Jeff, Jennifer, and Jason, have been for me that "working laboratory" that helps us grow right. And, of course, my family of origin has helped me grow—Mom and Dad, my two sisters, Marilyn and Barbara, and my brother, Roger, along with many other relatives. In addition, I mention the Raikkos, my in-laws, who have encouraged me to pursue my writing.

In addition, my thanks to a group of co-workers—George and Martie Sheffer, George and Jane Sheffer, Jim and Carol Groesbeck, and Dave Allen—who have been my working community for the past six years and have provided endless material for the book, due to their total commitment to the Lord and to helping young people and their families through the ministry of the Dale House. Thanks also goes to six years of paraprofessional training staff who gave their time as counselors to troubled young people. And thanks to the hundreds of families seeking help through the Dale House project who allowed me to participate in their healing.

Foreword

During my three years with Young Life in Colorado Springs, I became aware of a man who was quietly making an impact on the city. That man was Dr. James Oraker, familiarly known to all of us as Jim. Wherever I encountered him, whether he was sitting on the floor of the Dale House, playing his guitar, surrounded by troubled kids, or greeting a military officer whose daughter had run away, two qualities about him attracted me. One was his sensitivity to people: Jim is aware and respectful of the unique and distinct presence and potential of another person. The other quality was his ability to practically work out Biblical principles—in his counseling and practice as well as in his personal manner of life.

For some time I was aware of the value of this man's life and of his personal mission to help families nurture individual maturity. I felt that these qualities that I appreciated in him as a person also equipped him for a wider usefulness. I encouraged him—even urged him—to expand his working knowledge of the adolescent and the family into a manuscript that could be published and distributed. His would be a book reaching beyond the Dale House and Colorado Springs to other teenagers and their families; it would serve the Young Life staff, but it would go far beyond Young Life.

It was my privilege to work with Jim in the early stages of the planning for this book. Now, as a father of three teenagers, with a fourth turning thirteen soon, I am pleased to have the sensitive, practical counsel of Jim Oraker available to our family in book form.

This is not a book of theory, academic and untried; it is forged out of human lives—some that are working, some that are not. I highly recommend it to families who have children of all ages, families who are open to learning the highest human skill of all—the skill of parenting.

Jeb Stuart Magruder

Introduction

THE FAMILY: MODEL OF HOPE

Yes, the relationships in families are the juice of life, the longings, the frustrations, and intense loyalties. We get our strength from those relationships, we enjoy them, even the painful ones. Of course, we also get some of our problems from them, but the power to survive those problems comes from family too.

URIE BRONFENBRENNER
Psychology Today, May 1977

Child-development expert Urie Bronfenbrenner, sometimes called "the Family Man," notes that although families seem to be having their share of difficulties, they work far better than any other method of molding individual persons. As members of families, we seem to live in the tension of needing to be there and wanting to run away.

I work at a project for young people who are having difficulty coping with living. The Dale House project is sponsored by Young Life—an international organization whose purpose is sharing the message of Christ with high school young people. Staff members at the project communicate this message as they reach out to meet the painful needs of young people and their families. Three houses are staffed with counselors who are supervised and trained by a full-time clinical psychologist. A social-worker and two residential supervisors complete the project staff. The Dale House is a response by a group of Christians who are committed to impact the lives of thousands of searching young people.

When Danny (age 15) ran away and came to the Dale House, he ran away from his family. He didn't run away from school or from his job or from his girlfriend. He ran away from the people he was living with—his mom and dad, two sisters, and a brother.

When Art (age 42) ran away, he too ran away from his family. Oh, the job seemed to be supplying its share of pressure, but when we got underneath all of the excuses, Art, too, was running away from home.

Judy (age 26) ran away from home, too. Two kids in diapers and a husband who spent most of his time running around the country were more than she could handle. She spoke of no respect, no caring for her, and a life that seemed to have very little meaning; so she left.

And yet, we're told by Paul Tournier, the Swiss psychiatrist and author, that we all need a place to belong.[1] Robert Brain, anthropologist and author, writes in an article on friendship that our need to be cared for might very well be an instinct.[2] Everybody, says Brain, needs to be known and loved and cared for. It seems a little silly, then, doesn't it, to run away from home when home is the very place you most need to be? But then, maybe you've never experienced that overwhelming feeling that the *only* solution to your problem was to run away. Maybe you live in the type of family that cares deeply for its members and won't let them run away, a family where problems, even the toughest problems, are taken on as family issues, and the members stick together until they find a solution.

If, as some are saying, the family *is* the best social institution for making people, then the family of the future is the family where each member is cared for, and, in turn, each member reaches out and cares for others. Those suggesting alternative models to the family style of life had better approach the subject with a great deal of caution and respect for what has gone before them.

In his book *Love and Conflict*, Gibson Winter, clergyman, educator, and social ethicist, states that the family is the key to the very moral fiber of the society.[3] He says that once the healthy bonds fostered in families begin to crumble, the society will reflect this degeneration of relationships—for example, there is a general apathy and a breakdown of law and order; crime increases and vandalism begins to occur frequently at earlier and earlier ages; and health-care statistics reflect increasing numbers of those who are mentally ill.

For the Christian, the family just might be at the heart of God's intention for creation. We are told that we have certain mothering and fathering instincts, and we are also well aware of the biology of reproduction. It's a built-in function of our maleness and femaleness; as we reproduce, "the juices begin to flow" that alert each of us to the need for feeding and caring for our young ones.

Perhaps the family as God's order provides a special foundation for expressing God's intention for our lives.

Needless to say, the family is not perfect. Just as a family can be a most intimate and exciting place to grow, it can also be destructive. In my family counseling practice, I suppose I have encountered every possible type of man's inhumanity to man—child abuse, incest, rape, murder, physical violence, and many others. Yet, just when I think I've seen everything, I'm confronted with a new twist to human evil. Yes, some families are troubled and sick, others are nurturing and healthy, and some are just in-between. I am still convinced, however, that the family is our main hope and provides us with the basic structure for living out God's intention in our lives.

We as parents are responsible for teaching and bringing up our children in healthy ways. We are not, however, to load on ourselves the blame and guilt for all that happens to our sons and daughters. Families carry with them a great deal of risk, but that's the beauty of life. So, knowing that is true, we press on with the task of parenting, some of us in one-parent families resulting from death or divorce, others in families stricken by the grief of disease or accident, and others in families immobilized by emotional barriers which press to the breaking point. Those of us who have learned some skills must pass them on to equip other families in need; those of us with responsibilities in government must press for legislation giving families the resources needed to raise children in this day and age; those of us in ministerial positions must provide deep spiritual wells for families to draw from at all times.

WHAT FAMILY?

Yes, the family is a great hope in our society. It seems to be the living laboratory of life itself and a direct link to God's plan for our lives. What family? Yours and mine. That group of significant people we live with. That group which has shaped us from the beginning and has given us the very best they have to give—themselves. That family is the one you're reading about.

A BOOK ABOUT FAMILY

This book is about families. It's about ways to insure that healthy growth can take place, and that effective coping devices are developed, in *each member* of the family. I am hearing increasingly today about the need for effective methods of coping. Good, healthy people, it seems, come from all kinds of families—inner-city families, suburban families, ghetto families, one-parent families, older-parent families, and even no-parent families. At least one of the common threads woven into healthy children is that their families have learned how to cope with difficulties. These children have learned how to turn seemingly impossible situations into opportunities for their own growth and development. These are young people who have been taught not to quit, but to look for ways of conquering the seemingly impossible. These young people have been taught that they are valuable, that God created them for a special purpose and loves them and has their best interest in mind. These young people have learned to be responsible for their behavior, to initiate positive solutions rather than being passive, and to do their very best without taking advantage of another human being in order to somehow appear superior. These young people come from all kinds of families, and the family has been the key to their fulfillment.

I have decided, in this book, to focus primarily on the adolescent family, that is, a family with at least one adolescent member. These families will not all look alike. Some will have only one parent. Others will be blended families, uniting parents with children from previous marriages. Some will have a majority of small children, while others a majority of adolescents. Some will be facing seemingly impossible situations, while others will have smooth sailing. However, though each family has its own problems, it also will have its unique resources to deal with these problems. That is the reason that the family stands alone as unequalled in the task of making people. In a family where God's intention operates, people are important, and each situation is viewed from a point-of-view which sees the importance of the person, an ingredient which is missing in many institutional cases, or in disturbed families.

Most of us must realize that we will need help at some point. Being a family does not mean that we must "go it alone". The single parent has an especially tough job, as does a family in crisis. As individuals, and as the Church, we must learn to reach out to be a community of people who care enough to support these who have an extra load to carry. One widow told me, "I can never forget the Young Life leader who stepped into my son's life when he was left without a father at the age of 13. Or the business associate who opened up numerous opportunities for him to follow his vocation. There is no way the contribution of their practical kind of caring can ever be measured."

Much of my counseling is done with families who are having a difficult time with an adolescent, or with an adolescent who is having a difficult time with a family. I also work with many adolescents who have run away, who are experiencing legal problems, and who are trapped in a seemingly inescapable prison of drug use, sexual exploitation, or serious mental problems. This book deals with these situations as experienced in many different kinds of families.

Adolescence is a very important time for reflection, evaluation, and decisive movement toward the future. Parents are very important to adolescents, as are other family members, during this transition time in life. We who are resource people to families can be of great service to young people in those final years of preparation before they are on their own in the world. My desire is that this book be that kind of practical resource.

Some writers, mostly for humor I hope, talk about adolescence as a stage parents desperately pray will pass quickly, or joke that children should be buried at age 11 and dug up again at 18. It's dangerous to think this way. A family is in constant change. A family that contains a 6-year-old and a 36-year-old, ten years later has a 16-year-old and a 46-year-old. Neither of them is the same. Both for the parent and for the child, the task has changed. The parents of an adolescent need to be just as active, just as interested, and just as involved as they were when the young person was 6—but in a different way.

In his book *The First Three Years of Life*,[4] Burton White, Director of Harvard University's Pre-School Project, mentions three goals that parents need to attend to during those first three years: (1) to give love and affection; (2) to teach the skills that the child is ready to learn; and (3) to stimulate and provide for a curiosity concerning the world around the child. The goals for an adolescent are similar. Only the age has changed, and if a child has been taught well and the foundation has been laid for more love and affection, more skills, and more curiosity, the task of the adolescent parent is clear; that is, to continue to build on that foundation which was laid in childhood.

NOTES

1. Paul Tournier, *A Place for You* (New York: Harper & Row, 1968).
2. Robert Brain, "Somebody Else Should Be Your Own Best Friend," *Psychology Today*, October 1977, p. 123.
3. Gibson Winter, *Love and Conflict* (Garden City, N.Y.: Doubleday Dolphin Books, 1961), p. 27.
4. Burton White, *The First Three Years of Life* (Englewood Cliffs, N.J.: Prentice-Hall, 1975), p. 10.

1. Parents Are Important

At our house, we have a new-word list on the refrigerator. Any new word can be added to the list by our children Jeffrey (10) and Jennifer (9), if they know the definition. Some of our friends have been attracted to the list by such words as semen, menstruation, sperm, and Fallopian tube.

There are two reasons for these words. First, we have a new baby, and Jeff and Jennifer have been studying conception and birth for the past nine months. Second, it reflects our philosophy that preadolescent young people should be increasingly familiar with the natural growth and development of their bodies.

Often I encounter adults who find it very hard to accept the fact that many young people are ignorant of the physical growth and development surrounding puberty. Their understanding of what's going on in their emotions is even more disastrous. Our educational systems are now doing a fair job of sex education from the physical point of view, but the emotional aspect is relatively untouched. One recent study by Sylvia Hacker, Ph.D., who operates the University of Michigan's health clinic, concludes: "Sex education in U.S. schools has failed because courses concentrate on mechanical details of anatomy and reproduction, rather than emotional complexities of human relationships."

Dr. Hacker bases her conclusion on the steady increase in the number of unwanted pregnancies among teenagers at the same time that the national birth rate is declining in an age of "sexual enlightenment."

Typical concerns expressed to her by sexually experienced young people, ages 15 to 23, were: "What will she think if I try something?" and "How far shall I let him go?"

While those interviewed indicated a general desire to avoid pregnancy, they expressed varying degrees of self-consciousness about using contraceptives. "If you carry one with you," one girl said, "it's like you're asking for it."

"Sex and contraception," Dr. Hacker observes, "are still relatively taboo subjects in our post-Puritanical culture. Even the most liberal parents tend to view sex as a private matter, and the schools treat it as a dry academic subject. "As a result, the kids turn to their peers, where an enormous amount of mythology is still being perpetrated. For example, some believe you can't get pregnant 'the first time.' "

Dr. Hacker says, "What the kids really want to know about are human relationships." She feels that the situation cannot be improved in the schools until the adult population learns to discuss sex comfortably with young people. Only then, she says, can the schools properly "help youngsters get in touch with their own feelings and values."[1]

Many parents are "up in arms" if our institutions meddle in this sacred area. And I agree. The value system of a sexual relationship *is* a sacred area, one which I believe is best dealt with in the home. However, because most homes have failed miserably, the educational systems are being forced to step in and do something. I applaud their efforts at least to bring some order out of chaos.

John Conger, a psychologist researching adolescence, makes the observation that "the single most important factor . . . . in influencing whether the adolescent will emerge from the challenge of this period reasonably happy, self-confident, and prepared to meet the demands of an unpredictable future will be one's parents."[2] Believe it!

In other words, whether a young person is experiencing lots of trouble or sailing through adolescence seemingly unscarred, major significant people in the adventure are the parent, parents, or other primary caretakers. I support this concept wholeheartedly, and this book is written to any adult who is committed to being a significant person during, and immediately following, the years 9 to 17.

Hal Lyons, former director of HEW's program for the Gifted, reports: "I worked briefly with the White House task force on the gifted in 1968, and we went around the country interviewing some of the United States' most successful citizens. One of the things identified then that helps realize potential more than anything else was some person, a teacher or coach or some other respected adult who dropped his whole mask and rank and status and entered a one-to-one relationship. . . ."[3]

In counseling families in trouble, I find parents laboring under various burdens of being a parent to an adolescent. Some feel laden with *guilt*—"What have I done?" or "If I only could do it over again"; laden with *fear*—"If I can just keep him away from that crowd," or "I hope drugs don't trap my daughter"; laden with *apathy*—"They are on their own now, I can do no more," or "Let 'em learn the hard way"; or laden with *hopelessness*—"It's too late, I must concentrate on the other members of the family."

Other parents have little need to seek counseling, but they would appreciate some direction with their young family members. This book is written to any parent wanting to understand this stage of growth better and to make it an exciting time of life for the teenager and for the other members of the family as well. Realize that you, the parents, are very significant to the proper development of the young person. The family is a factory that produces people, and your own growth will be richer if you enter this period with enthusiasm and hope.

Dr. John Claypool pastor of Northminster Baptist Church, Jackson, Mississippi, says:

> There is a word every parent needs to hear during the adolescent era of their child's life. Just as a seed disappears for a period of time, and you begin to fear that it is lost altogether, so there is a time in a child's life when it seems that all the efforts of the parents are for nothing. Not so! If there has been a faithful sowing of the seed during the long days and nights of childhood, a harvest of healthy personhood will likely emerge. This does not mean that one's children will come out carbon copies of their parents, for this would ill equip them for living in their own day. Rather, it means they will be able to cope creatively and responsibly with life, which is all any parent should want.[4]

It seems pretty well accepted that patterns in the personality begun during the early years of life will continue to develop through adolescence. If, therefore, there is some reason to believe that all is not going well, it probably is a good idea to check it out. It doesn't take too long for a qualified counselor to pinpoint problems that need intervention, and often you can prevent a great deal of misery in the future. Once these problems are diagnosed, you can go about solving them and make the adjustment to adulthood a whole lot easier for your child.

You can count on three important influences or shifts hitting at full force during early adolescence. These shifts are biological, social, and intellectual. I call these influences *shifts* because there really is little new about them. They have been there all along, but somewhere between the ages of 9 and 17 they become very accelerated. Each of these shifts will have a dramatic effect on all of the areas of growth and development of the adolescent.

Adolescence is a socially defined developmental period. In the United States, people are considered adolescents from about the age of 11 or 12 until they are able to assume full responsibility for themselves. In our culture, this point is not well defined, and some young adults "hang on" to their parents much longer than is healthy. One mother, rather desperate, recently told me of her 23-year-old who appears for every meal, contributes nothing to the family emotionally or financially, and doesn't work. He is selfish and presumptuous, but he is her son and it's hard to ignore him or kick him out.

This sad situation finds its roots often in the troubling 1960s. John J. Conger has commented on the "fall out" from these confusing times, suggesting that many young people were brought into a fantasy of instant and painless happiness and joy, only to be left behind. "Many of the adolescents of the 1960s," says Conger, "who now as young adults find themselves struggling outside the social order as drug users, defeated dropouts, or armed revolutionaries on the run, would have found other alternatives had they not grown up in the middle and late 1960s in explosive, unstable, polarized communities. Never before, at least to my knowledge, have so many brilliant, promising, ex-high-school valedictorians, 4H club leaders, and the like ended up as social outcasts, and for such atypical and frequently tragic reasons."[5]

Like any other stage of development, adolescence is a time best suited for the accomplishment of certain tasks:

- Adjustment to the physical changes of puberty and later adolescent growth and to the flood of new subjective impulses brought on by sexual maturity.
- Development of independence from parents or other caretakers.
- Establishment of effective social and working relationships with same- and opposite-sex peers, including experimenting in the area of vocation.
- And, in the midst of the others, the development of a system of values and a sense of identity.

All of these tasks must be accomplished within the framework of the three major shifts: (1) the biological change ushering in puberty; (2) an intellectual shift bringing about new abilities to think and to reason; and (3) a social shift, which finds the young person strongly influenced by a peer culture.

Like any other stage of development, adolescence has a beginning and an end. Certain things happen to start it, and at some point the person finishes adolescence and enters the adult stage of growth. While the beginning is both cultural and biological, it is most dramatically biological. It may be marked by things like this: Barbara is 10 and already she is aware of softer curves in her body. Mom buys her a bra and encourages her to be grown up and to model her behavior after young girls older than she. John is 11 and into sports. He is somewhat interested in girls, but a little self-conscious that he is small and that he has little pubic hair and his penis seems underdeveloped.

It is generally agreed that adolescence begins in biology and ends in culture. Of course, biological and cultural differences exist throughout adolescence, but it is biology that alerts the child to prepare for other changes—in thinking, in motive, in feeling or acting. In short, a new combination has been unlocked, and it is normal for the person to react to events in a new way.

One thing that impresses me about my children is their confidence in handling life's situations with ease and authority. I have the distinct impression that our 9-year-old can handle any situation that comes her way. She knows how to upset her 10-year-old brother; she's a master at wrapping her father around her little finger; she's successful at coming between Mom and Dad; and she's equally successful at finding an impeccable system of logic for almost anything her little heart desires.

I am convinced, however, that Jennifer is in for a definite and exciting awakening. Life, which is rather predictable for her now, will take on dramatic changes. Moods now colored in hues of grey, brown, yellow, and green will explode into wild reds and oranges, overwhelmingly soft pastels, brilliant purples and blues. Fragrances will delight her sense of smell and taste, and textures and sensations she had no idea existed will burst into her everyday life. Feelings of sadness, sorrow, and rejection will also cause her to hit new lows. In the cold, technical jargon of psychology, Jennifer will biologically become an adolescent. This initial change is called puberty.

What then should a parent strive for during these important years of adolescence? John Conger gives us some important advice: "Today . . . parents can under favorable circumstances provide for their children models of successful, autonomous, flexible, problem-solving behavior, and they can provide love and a fundamental underlying security; but they cannot provide detailed blueprints for mastering the changing demands of a society in headlong transition."[6]

Maybe the goal of being an effective model is the highest priority for a parent. Closely following are providing an atmosphere of love and affection; encouraging and affirming individual gifts and skill development; and providing opportunities for success and failure, for new learning and understanding about the larger world. Although I can't possibly teach my child everything about life because of the vast knowledge explosion, I can teach my child how to solve problems, deal with conflict, cope with stress and disappointment, and develop a deep spirituality that gives stability and meaning to life.

Yes, parents are important for better or for worse. They are probably that single most important factor in the development of an effective person. This is in light of the belief stated by H. J. Eysenck, noted scientist and author, that the factors impacting the human personality are about three-fourths heredity and one-fourth environmental.[7] In stressing the importance of parents I am also acknowledging that the one-fourth environment can have dramatic effects on some people. It certainly does play an important role in how all of us make use of the raw materials we have been given. Dr. Eysenck goes on to warn people not to misunderstand this general statement. The importance of heredity and environment will vary with different individuals, and the neglect of either would be foolish.

Dr. Lee Travis, the first Dean of the Fuller School of Psychology and an important person in my life, in a personal conversation, compared life to an airplane trip. You get on at one point and get off at another, said Dr. Travis. You can get up and move around a little within the airplane, but really not much. There is, however, a definite difference between a delightful trip and a miserable trip, and certain factors—crying babies, spilled coffee, pleasant flight attendants, stereo music, and the like—contribute to either your comfort or your misery.

In life, though we do not change our basic personalities much during our span of years, there is a vast difference between a challenging, expanding, and meaningful life, and a bitter, angry, restricted, and disappointing life. The difference seems to be how we adapt to our situations, how we handle or cope with unexpected change or stress. That ability to adapt, to handle a negative situation in a positive way, is very much a gift from our parents. To say this in spiritual terms, if you give your children only two things in life, please give them a sound faith and an ability to apply it in all situations.

NOTES

1. Sylvia Hacker, "Sex-Ed Not So Hot, Says Ph.D.," *Extra!*, November 1977.
2. John J. Conger, "Current Issues in Adolescent Development," in Supplement 1334 to *Masters Lectures on Developmental Psychology* (Journal Supplement Abstract Service of the American Psychological Association), p. 8.
3. Cited in *MGM Pipelines*, May 1974. The original interviews were conducted by the White House Task Force on the Gifted, 1968, under the direction of Hal Lyons, Director of HEW's Program for the Gifted.
4. John Claypool, "Sowing and Praying: Warning and Promise" (sermon given on January 15, 1978), Northminster Baptist Church, Jackson, Mississippi.
5. Conger, p. 12.
6. Conger, p. 13.
7. Eysenck, H. J., *Psychology Is About People* (LaSalle, Ill.: Open Court, 1972), p. 38.

2. Biological Change

It has been said that adolescence begins in biology and ends in culture. The period seems to divide into two major phases, with a transitional period overlapping the beginning and the end. I have decided to use ages 10–13 and 16–20 as the ranges of these two phases, with the transitional period as age 14–15. The earliest, and perhaps most dramatic, change is biological—a physiological development with strong emotional overtones.

It is essential to point out that, despite widespread opinion that they are all similar, all adolescents are not alike. They do not face the same problems, nor do they respond to them in the same way. What is true is that all young people do experience bodily changes, and all must face the challenge of becoming independent and self-supportive, but their approach to this challenge, their resources for meeting it, and their developmental timetable may vary considerably.

Most of the remarkable physical changes occur during early adolescence, between 10 and 15 years of age. In females, the normal signs of puberty are breast development, appearance of pubic and axillary hair, enlargement of the lips surrounding the vagina, and a sudden increase in height. In males, puberty is accompanied by an increase in body height, enlargement of the penis and scrotum, and growth of pubic and axillary hair. Puberty ends when the person is physiologically capable of reproducing children, a condition that usually precedes legal adulthood by several years.

Biological sexual maturity brings the first occurrence of menstruation for girls, and for boys the appearance of live spermatozoa in the urine and the first ejaculation of semen. Along with these biological changes comes a wide spectrum of emotional responses—fear, embarrassment, excitement, confusion, disgust, awe, inferiority, anxiety, and others.

The often unpredictable combination of physiological and emotional forces challenges every parent. It is a good time to check out your family atmosphere and take steps to update it if you want to provide the best support system for the development of a healthy concept of sexuality in your children. The manner in which a family deals with physical changes and sexual awareness at this stage will greatly influence the quality of each family member's attitude toward sexuality for the rest of their lives. The healthy integration of feelings in this area, like all healthy growth, requires a willingness to work at it.

PHASE I

From the first flowing of the hormones, life takes on a new dimension of emotions. If you could get inside your teenager's thoughts, you would be very likely to hear: "My desires are different. My attitudes are different. My emotions are different. I'm bewildered by my sexual feelings. I've never felt anything before like this intensity!" Confusion is characteristic of the early phase (Phase 1) of biological change. Feelings are developing that have never been thought about before. It will take some time for a balance to develop between feeling and thinking.

It's a sobering realization that many adolescents reach this stage in development with virtually no correct information or with inadequate coping devices to deal with this new emotional flood. That's why the behavior of young people is often driven by embarrassment, fear, exploitation, or fantasy. They are ignorant about what's going on. If you have not spent the first nine years preparing your child for puberty, you have lost valuable time, and you'll have a great deal of ground to cover quickly. Here's an example of what happened in one family where there was a negative kind of help.

Linda is now 15. She was raised in a strict religious environment, with long lists of do's and don't's. This led her to assume that perfect conformity to this code was the goal. What she picked up about sex was negative from the beginning, with the genital areas seen as "dirty," therefore "bad." Sexual development was dealt with sarcastically rather than from the point of giving information.

On top of this, when she was 9 years old, Linda was confronted with sexual advances from her uncle. She still remembers the intense, ambiguous feelings of fear and sinfulness mixed with sexual excitement. Her sense of pleasure thoroughly confused her. She hated herself. Because of her terrible fear and guilt, she would not talk with her parents, yet she repeated the act with her uncle on several occasions because of the extreme pleasure aroused in her body.

At age 13, Linda "turned her first trick" for cash and became involved sexually with a number of men. It was not unusual for her to "party" on Friday and Saturday nights; then out of desperation she would scrub up for Sunday morning church in an attempt to atone for her "sin." She was developing a deep hatred for men, and took advantage of every opportunity to humiliate them, sexually tease them, or promote jealousy between two of the men she was servicing.

By age 15, Linda has had three abortions, has been deeply involved with drugs, and has been in and out of several psychiatric institutions because of her inability to manage her emotions. Obviously, it would be an oversimplification to say that Linda's whole problem stems from the fact that she was not helped to understand biological development or to cope with the intense feelings resulting from biological change. But Linda's story is an example, however extreme, of the devastating style of behavior that can result from lack of preparation for these biological changes and their accompanying emotions.

Linda's sexual confusion, of course, was intensified by the encounters with her uncle. While she might have dared talk with her parents about normal sexual excitement, her uncle's threats, along with the knowledge that her parents thought highly of him, made it impossible for her to explain her discomfort around him. She was totally overcome by guilt, shame, and excitement and dealt with it by concluding that she was a "bad," worthless girl.

Things might have been different if Linda's parents had been more understanding of what was happening to her biologically. As Linda began puberty, she became a different person. Vague body sensations, which probably gave her added energy at age 8 or 9, suddenly became strong erratic or aggressive impulses clamoring for expression.

This first phase of biological change, ending somewhere in the middle teens, is strongly influenced by natural instinct. Sexual fantasies and feelings resulting in pleasure, guilt, shame, or confusion are not uncommon. These fantasies can be so overwhelming that they may keep the young person from talking to anyone about them.

A great deal of energy can be expended in an attempt to control and maintain these feelings. The boy or girl may spend time alone, thinking or daydreaming, in an effort to figure out these feelings. This isolation may, in turn, cause parents concern, especially when it is accompanied by a sudden lack of progress, even in determination, in school.

Dale, another teenager, was shocked and felt polluted when he had his first "wet dream" (nocturnal emission). He was further ridden with guilt by discovering that, by manipulating his own genitals, he could produce this ejaculation, which was accompanied by an exciting and pleasant sensation. He began wondering if God would ever forgive him for this act of self-pleasing. Rather than seeking sexual encounters with others, he began to withdraw from social contacts into his own predictable self-eroticism. He developed a rich fantasy life in which he became the hero, not only in sexual conquests, but in normal living situations as well. He imagined himself as the athletic hero, the much sought after male companion of attractive females, and a person with great wealth and success.

More and more the pleasures of masturbation became a strong and controlling occupation. His fantasy life took precedence over any other enjoyments, and he became more and more an isolated person. He felt overwhelmed with his own inadequacies, and his disturbing sense of guilt soon pervaded every area of his life. As his concentration level diminished, his grades went down and he began dropping out of his extracurricular activities.

Like Linda, Dale represents a group of young people who are flabbergasted by the intensity of feelings during early biological changes. It would not be fair to say of Dale that his problems would have been totally eliminated if he had been informed adequately of his biological development. It is, however, a striking example of what can happen to a young person who does not have proper guidance, and the resulting maturity, to handle these strong sexual feelings.

Most young people will end up somewhere between Linda's acting out or Dale's isolation. Those I talk with usually do not demonstrate severe sexual problems. However, they do reveal a great deal of ignorance about what is happening in their bodies. Such misinformation often causes them to be anxious, fearful, and to develop destructive sexual relationships.

The confusion accompanying this early phase of biological change is often unsettling to the young person. The young man, previously indifferent to his undergarments, for instance, can suddenly find himself having sexual fantasies or feelings of pleasure, guilt, and shame as he dresses and undresses. These feelings, intense and sudden, can break through at inappropriate, unexpected times in impulsive behavior. When this kind of thing happens, the young person can appear irritable or edgy and may become argumentative or seemingly rebellious. For the most part, this is due to extra energy expended in an effort to control these new, strong feelings. Parents, focusing on the overt behavior only, may entirely miss the intense struggle going on at a different level.

In Linda's case, she was unable to cope with her guilt, pleasure, anger, and desire to please her parents. She went to church to get rid of her guilt. She "cashed in" on sexual favors to get back at her uncle. She slept with many men out of a deep need to be held and accepted. She was at the mercy of her emotions, and when she desperately needed a friend or a parent to confide in, she isolated herself and tightly guarded her secret for fear of rejection and severe criticism.

When her parents did begin to put together this puzzle of sexual adventure her fears were realized. She received both rejection and severe criticism.

What Linda needed as she approached puberty was some help in understanding that she was going to begin feeling new emotions, that she should expect feelings that would be very strong at times. She needed a parent to talk to, a friend to confide in—someone who knew how to listen and had her best interest in mind. In the context of confidence she could ask "dumb" questions like, "Do you get pregnant by kissing?"

During Phase I of biological change, parents need to exercise a great deal of patience in order to provide the young person with an atmosphere for thinking through these feelings. Remember that feelings often predominate during this phase, resulting in impulsive actions based on poor judgments. Some parents respond by spending a lot of time at the school, in a counselor's office, or venting their frustrations over the phone to friends. Some wonder if their young person will ever get out of this phase.

Here are some suggestions for parents who want to create a helpful learning experience for early adolescents:

- Remember the importance of spending time together talking, sharing, or doing activities you both enjoy.
- Go to a movie together and share your impressions of the movie by talking about it together.
- If and when it seems appropriate, ask directly about feelings of attraction to the opposite sex, fantasies, or questions that are being raised.
- Share what you recall of your own adolescent struggles and solutions, remembering they are yours and may not match those of your young person at all.

• Be willing to talk about alternative ways of coping with the difficult situations your son or daughter is facing.

PHASE II

During Phase II, from age 16 to 20, the balance of power shifts from impulsive behavior and overwhelming feelings to more ability to reason and think about feelings. Feelings are still intense; but the young person has learned how to let them surface, to listen to them and consider carefully what action should be taken. While this may sound simple and ideal, for most it is not. Many young people often continue to be too impulsive in their actions, while others are entirely too analytical about their feelings. In fact, their thinking seems to keep them from acting. During Phase II, however, a greater balance will be achieved between reasoning and impulsive action.

One example of the shift is seen in the difference between many 14- to 15-year-olds, and the 16- to 17-year-olds I know at Dale House. Almost nothing I say to the 15-year-old sinks in, no matter how true it is: "Drugs will trap you in a false reality." "People will use you on the street." "If you drop out of school, you may be very sorry later and want to go back." "Running away from your problems never solves them."

Most 17-year-olds we see have been out on the street and have been forced to consider their predicament. They have learned the hard way. The younger adolescent has too many "juices" flowing to reason very well. That, coupled with trouble at home, often results in action swayed by emotional impulse and not well thought through.

Several things seem to contribute to the shift from Phase I to Phase II:

- The hormonal and biological processes stabilize.
- The fear and panic of beginning puberty diminish with the further development of the thinking and understanding capacity.
- There is a shift away from parents as the only close love object. At the same time, parents become less directive and more of a consultant, providing time to think, talk, and plan with the young person.

If I were to illustrate the phases of biological change it would look like this:

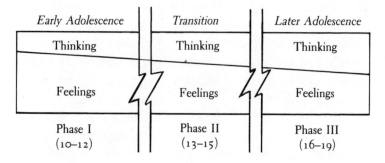

Early Adolescence		Transition		Later Adolescence
Thinking		Thinking		Thinking
Feelings		Feelings		Feelings
Phase I (10–12)		Phase II (13–15)		Phase III (16–19)

EFFECTS OF BIOLOGICAL CHANGE

It is normal for most young people to wonder if they are normal. They look around and measure themselves against other young people their age. They read books about the "average adolescent" and wonder why they aren't average. *It is very important to emphasize that physical development and sexual maturation among young people varies widely within the normal range of development.*

This concern for normality represents one of the many questions facing a young person. Marked bodily changes initiate emotional conflicts of varying intensity. Some are resolved quite easily, and others seem insurmountable. Many of these conflicts revolve around the young person's identity. The body seems either to rapidly change or not to change nearly fast enough; the young person is either flooded with changes related to sexual maturation or feels left out. In either case, the individual tries to make sense out of this and to be realistic about hopes and desires for the final product. Of course, "body image" is not a simple aspect of life. A young man judged attractive by nearly all who encounter him may *feel* unattractive because of earlier experiences. A young woman excessively concerned with her skin, her hair, or her figure may feel ugly even though she is looked on by others as quite beautiful.

Maturation rates vary widely among normal adolescents. One boy at age 15 may be small with no pubertal development, whereas another boy at the same age may appear to be virtually a grown man. Late maturation for both men and women seems to cause greater emotional difficulty than does early maturation. Though there are no physical consequences to late maturation, late maturing men and women are often judged less attractive, less poised, and more "immoderate" in their behavior. They tend to engage in more attention-getting behavior; they are apt to be more restless, talkative, and bossy; they may be less popular with their peers; and fewer of them are leaders. This difference has been known to last for a long period of time.

Emotional conflicts related to the biological changes of adolescence often focus around menstruation for young women, nocturnal emissions for young men. The conflicts surrounding menstruation can best be handled by wise and understanding parents who (1) explain to their daughter the naturalness of this phenomenon; (2) show pride and pleasure in her greater maturity; and (3) see that she receives adequate medical care in case of physical difficulties. The mother particularly can make this a happy time, highlighting her daughter's future sexual and social role as a woman.

To a lesser degree, young men are concerned by nocturnal emissions, the ejaculation of seminal fluid during sleep. It seems true that the better informed young men are, the less they worry about this event and the less they tend to exaggerate its importance among their peers. Nevertheless, many young men do not receive proper instruction from their parents or from their peers, and therefore torture themselves with unnecessary fears.

How physical changes are prepared for and handled is a major matter for both the young person and the parents. These changes can initiate excellent opportunities for self-confidence to develop, or they can bring about confusion, feelings of inferiority, and self-doubt. One major consideration for every parent preparing younger children for the biological changes of adolescence is adequate sex education in the home. A general guideline for this education might go something like this: (1) during infancy, enjoy lots of holding, hugging, touching your baby, with great care given not to imply that certain parts of the body are "bad" or "dirty." (2) About age 4, begin age-graded information related to anatomy, physiology, and sexuality. These programs should carefully prepare the child for accurate and specific information, including conception and birth, and should be completed before age 9. (3) By age 9, or slightly before, introduce the subject of puberty, and discuss it at both a physiological and an emotional level—again in a climate of warmth and acceptance.

For every individual, the subject of sex education has physical, emotional, and ethical implications. It is a subject about real people and real relationships that I believe is best taught in the home. Unfortunately, many families can only treat the subject with embarrassment and with very little balance.

They do not give physical and emotional information accurately; nor do they treat moral considerations in a manner that provides any positive link to life and creation as things of beauty. If you feel that you have neglected any, or all, efforts at sex education in the hope that your adolescent would learn on his or her own, it may be in your best interest to admit your failure right now, and start taking steps to fill in the gaps as soon as possible.

3. Sexuality

Sexuality, so flaunted and even worshipped in our day, is frequently spoken of and lived out in the Bible. The biblical "greats" were men and women of earthly passions, who had to make choices about their sexual desires, even as about their urge to worship. Abraham decided to sleep with his wife's servant girl.[1] Isaac's wife was so attractive that he told the Philistine men she was his sister because he thought they would kill him to get her for themselves. This strategy worked well until the king looked out the window one day and saw Isaac "fondling" Rebekah.[2] Jacob fell in love with Rachel, who was "shapely, and in every way a beauty," and worked fourteen years in order to win her as his wife.[3] David, pacing the palace roof one sleepless night, saw a "woman of unusual beauty taking her evening bath." He sent for her and lay with her, and made her pregnant.[4] His involvement led him to have the woman's husband killed. "But the Lord was very displeased," the Scripture records, "with what David had done." The two spies that Joshua sent into Jericho stopped overnight at the house of a prostitute, Rahab, who protected them from their pursuers,[5] and who is named in the line of Christ.

If sexuality is a God-given part of being human, then there must be clues in the Bible regarding its proper expression. The men and women just mentioned evidently had as much of a problem using their sexuality properly as we have today. Yet, the Scriptures give us many guidelines. Lewis Smedes a Professor of Ethics at Fuller Seminary, Pasadena, California, writes in his book, *Sex For Christians,* "The gospel of Jesus Christ is good news for the whole person; so the gospel must be good news for us in our befuddled attempts to live with our sexuality. If Christ promises hope, it must include hope for a better sexual life. Our sexuality is woven too thoroughly into the garment of our lives to be left out of life's renewal in Christ. For this reason, our relationship to Jesus Christ cannot mean salvation from sexuality, nor can it mean only some new rules for the sexual game. We must receive the word of the gospel as the word of grace and freedom. And, in doing so, we must by all means understand that grace is not against nature but only against distortions of nature. Grace does not put sexuality down; it raises sexuality up into the service of the spirit. For this reason the grace of God must be the grace that liberates our sexuality as a power for love."[6]

Relating directly to our sexual nature, the gospel liberates us to experience what Smedes calls "the human drive toward intimate communion."[7] Smedes calls for "personal sexuality" as a prime expression of an adequate biblical view. Personal sexuality is best characterized by *having the other person's best interest in mind.* Smedes describes a spectrum[8] that places "functional sex" at one extreme, and "personal sexuality" at the other extreme. Functional sex is selfish and has no regard for the other as a person. While prostitution is one example, functional sex is also common in dating, courtship, living together experimentally, and even after years of marriage.

Personal sexuality has the interest and fulfillment of the other person in mind. It is a relationship of caring and love. The sex act becomes, then, a part of a deep and ongoing relationship which, according to Scripture (I Corinthians 7:25), is to be experienced within the context of marriage. Smedes insists that "Sexual fulfillment is achieved when a personal relationship underpins the genital experience, supports it, and sustains a human sexual relationship after it."[9]

Scripture indicates that the sex act was intended by God to be part of a quality relationship. It is a bond between two people who are committed in love to each other for life. Thus, the sex act is part of God's intended order (Genesis 2:24) to be enjoyed. It is a sensitive, giving, serving part of relationship, consistent with the biblical view of love. It promotes wholeness in the marriage relationship.

In the Bible the human being is viewed as an integrated whole—a unity including the intellectual, emotional, physical, and spiritual. A person's sexuality is a significant part of that wholeness.

Sexuality is built into our flesh and blood. We all have it, though hormone changes will intensify it significantly at early adolescence. Both infant males and infant females are capable of sexual responsiveness (erection and lubrication) at birth. Despite the myth that sexual responsiveness is a mystery, it is very much a physiological reality.

The Bible has directives about the dangers of sexual promiscuity.[10] These rules have been questioned throughout history and we can only speculate on their complete meaning. They have been called punitive, irrelevant, stuffy, outdated, and not "hip." Nevertheless, they continue to be the heritage of our society, which is, on one side, selfish, abusive, and sexually exploitive; and, on the other side, capable of deeply loving, generous, and nurturing relationships. There is a great deal of wisdom in the guidelines of Scripture that many are missing because of their reactions to their personal situations—homes, parents, and so on.

THE FORCE OF SEX

Sex is one of the most powerful forces in the world. Men have given up thrones, women have overthrown personal careers, and people of all ages continue to forsake family and friends to pursue it. The dynamics of sexuality in relationships can be constructive and meaningful. However, a person's sexual pattern can also be a symptom of other personal problems; some examples follow.

Danny had fallen in love. Deborah, "his girl," was showing an interest in him. He felt different around her—special. He also felt he had to impress her. He watched her carefully to see if she laughed at the right time. He checked to see if she was watching mainly him. When she was, he felt important, like a man. He kept checking. When she watched other guys, his stomach sank a little and he found himself doing something, anything, to recapture her attention—a joke, a sarcastic remark. When she looked back at him, he felt important again.

Recently he had noticed strong desires to hold her, to touch her breasts. "I wonder if she would let me; that would really show she was mine." Dan was different at home; he day-dreamed a lot, and at night he fantasized about himself and Deborah. In his fantasies, he was with her and she always thought he was great. She held him, rubbed his back, and asked him if he would "turn her on." His fantasies often ended in masturbation, and after that he felt lonely.

Joan had fallen for Jim, who already had a girlfriend. She heard they were very involved with each other. She would do anything to be with him, but it seemed hopeless, so she settled for what she could get. When other guys would hold her and "feel her up," she imagined that she was in Jim's arms. She felt loved. She was a woman. Of course, he would probably never give her a chance, but she could really show him if he would let her. She knew what it meant to be a woman. She would do anything for him if he would only let her. More and more her life revolved around Jim, or at least around thinking about him.

Bob's parents were worried about him. He was staying out late at night, and he was less interested in being with the family. One Friday afternoon Bob's mother came home from town early and heard noise in Bob's room. She swung open the door and came face-to-face with Bob and Laura, nude and in each other's arms. She was shocked, and found herself yelling at the top of her lungs. Laura turned nonchalantly and said, "What's with her?" Bob was upset. He told Laura to get dressed and told his mother to leave. Later, when they came out of the room, Bob told his mother never to "stick her nose in his business again." For her part, what she saw was a confirmation of what she had suspected. Having to admit that it was happening was the shock, for she desperately had hoped it wasn't true. It was. Another nagging hurt was the jealousy she felt. She longed for the tenderness and passion that had disappeared from her own marriage years before.

Mrs. Jackson, divorced and unsettled, had recently arranged for her son, Barry, to move in with his girlfriend, Karen. Barry was 16, Karen 15. Mrs. Jackson thought it was time for Barry to learn some things about living with another person, in this case a female. She knew that Barry had not been the easiest person to live with. At some point in his life, he had better realize that, too. And maybe he could learn some things about sex. This seemed better than the way most kids learned—half-true stories from their friends. Besides, if he was going to learn about sex, he might as well face the realities that go along with it—the 24-hour, food-on-the-table type realities. He'd probably be home in a week or two.

Mr. Smith demanded that his 15-year-old daughter come and see me for counseling. She had just had an abortion and wanted to continue seeing her boyfriend, who was in the Army and was still married to a woman in St. Louis. He claimed he was getting a divorce, but it would take time. Mr. Smith was livid with anger. They could hardly say two words to each other without a barrage of name calling and accusations.

David ran away from home with his girlfriend, Lisa. Both were 15 and tired of their parents sermonizing and laying down rules on what they could and could not do. They were in love and just wanted to be with each other. They had sexual intercourse, but they were careful, always taking extra care to prevent conception. "We know what we are doing. Besides we are far more in love than our parents are." "Parents, that's a joke! I wonder if they ever enjoy each other's bodies— or have time for it. They are so uptight."

Then there was Steve, who "made it" with every "impor-tant" girl at school—the school stud. Beverly had a great body but was known as a girl not interested in sex. She was a challenge and a curiosity to Steve. After a few dates with

her, Steve "made some moves," and Beverly looked him
straight in the eye and said, "If that's what you want, I'm
not interested. I want a friend first and then sometime maybe
we can talk about more involvement. I'm a person, Steve, I
don't want to be used." A friend! Steve realized for the first
time that he didn't even know what that meant. To him
life was to be bargained for. You gave a little, got a little.
No one got hurt. What's the big deal?

To Beverly it was a big deal. Steve was telling her things
she had no sympathy with. He was out to get something
for Steve, and that made her sick. He was phony, self-centered,
and a liar. No way was she going to act like a "thing."

The stories are endless. What can we do with them? Are
there guidelines for parents wanting to help their children
develop a healthy sexuality? The rest of this chapter and the
next consider some of these guidelines.

SEX IN OUR TIME

Starting with the Kinsey Report[11] back in the late 1940s,
and continuing through Masters and Johnson[12] in the 1960s
and on to *The Hite Report*[13] in the 1970s, every detail of
sexual activity has been queried, documented, and distributed.
To say nothing of the popular magazines, such as *Playboy,
Cosmopolitan,* and others, which publish what people will
buy. These magazines, along with surveys and reports on current sex trends, help define the public mind, i.e., what people
are thinking about sex.

The meaning and use of sex is of universal curiosity. The
media try to convince us of its newness, whereas ancient writ-
ings suggest there is nothing new. It does, however, seem
to hold constant new adventure in relationships. Comments

about the joy of sex from older men and women—those in their seventies, eighties, and even nineties—can be heard. Amazingly rewarding things happen and new understandings are gained after three or four decades of marriage. There is always more to be discovered; not only physically, but for the whole person.

It is necessary for us to look at sex in our time, and to share with our children new insights that emerge out of our present world view.

Says Shere Hite, Columbia University doctoral student, in the popular survey, *The Hite Report:*

> We are currently in a period of transition, although it is unclear as yet to what. The challenge for us now is to devise a more humane society, one that will implement the best of the old values, like kindness and understanding, cooperation, equality, and justice throughout every layer of public and private life—a metamorphosis to a more personal and humanized society. Specifically, in sexual relations—we can again reopen many options. All the kinds of physical intimacy that were channeled into our one mechanical definition of sex can now be . . . rediffused throughout our lives.[13]

And I would add that the biblical view sees sex as much more than a mechanical act. From the sharing of warm body contact and simple forms of touching to the intimacy of the spirit that can occur through the sharing of a musical expression, going through a crisis together, a sudden coming upon a mountain stream, being closely present at a moment of grief, seeing a field of red poppies, hearing the crashing waves against the shore, the incredible bowing before the Almighty with words or without. Intimacy in a biblical sense is shared life, not the mere mechanical sexual techniques of personal gratification. It is a piece of yourself you give to another person. The two of you have something in common—each other.

Sex in our time is comprised of the three concepts of *love*, *sex*, and *sexuality*.

THREE TERMS: LOVE, SEX, SEXUALITY

Love is not simple to define. It is not easy to tell someone how love feels, how to make it happen, and how to keep it fresh. One thing becomes more sure as the years pass in a person's life: love is not automatic. It is developed within a relationship that allows for intimacy. It takes time. And it requires a definite choice—a decision by two people to be faithful to, and involved with, each other. The old marriage vows, so disregarded by many today, did cover well this idea that love grows in a climate of faithfulness. This is a faithfulness that respects the emotions, desires, and dreams of each person, and works toward communicating these in wisdom and understanding. The biblical view of love is that of a decision; a commitment as well as an attraction. It is more than a warm feeling; it is a responsibility and service to one another.

Sex could be described as intimate physical contact for pleasure, to share pleasure with another person or to experience it alone. It can be contact to the point of orgasm or ejaculation, complete genital intercourse, or physical handling. It has been said that if you put two young people—sexually mature but naive, who are somewhat attracted to each other—in a room by themselves, it wouldn't take long for them to figure how to express themselves in physical acts. Sex can be described explicitly; it can be taught. It can happen in a brief period of time, almost anyplace. And it can be done with little or no regard for a relationship that will continue. Sex has to do with physical expression and is usually seen as a physical act.

Sexuality, as we will use the term, involves all the characteristics of being male or female, personality as well as anatomy. It takes into consideration the whole person—mental, emotional, spiritual, and social, as well as physical, responses. It is also the product of culture, both societal and familial.

Sexuality, then, is more than genital activity. It is a relational power that includes sensitivity, warmth, openness, understanding, compassion, and mutual support. It is that aspect of personhood that makes us capable of entering into loving relationships—the gift of one's self to another. As mentioned earlier, problematical sexuality can be a symptom pointing to other problems; for example, self-centeredness, insecurity, fear, feelings of worthlessness, and self-destructive behavior.

In my opinion, healthy sexuality in young people is a major concern because it indicates a healthy person. To set the stage for healthy sexuality, we must enable our young people to know how to develop a healthy relationship with another person in all the aspects of human interaction. Though our children hopefully have been brought up in an atmosphere of love, as teenagers they are dealing with a new ingredient of intense sexual desire. Despite the continual flood of information, ignorance is still a chief problem with today's adolescents. For many, the what's and why's of sexual functioning, its pleasures, its pain, and its emotional and physical consequences are relatively unknown. Now they must be helped to comprehend what a healthy, warm, loving sexuality means. How does a parent go about helping in this very sensitive, intimate task?

SOME GUIDELINES FOR PARENTS

A. Begin to educate your children at about age 4 about anatomy and physiology. One of the sophisticated ways parents try to dodge this responsibility is by a disingenuous belief in nature and biological evolution: "Well, nature will take its course as it always has, and I don't want to meddle with my child's sexuality." NOT SO. The human teaching process must include passing on specific facts—those we have already discussed—and personal family guidelines as well.

Because our family was expecting the arrival of a new baby, we had been studying about conception, development, and birth. So that we might be more aware of their level of understanding, Judy and I asked Jeffrey and Jennifer to write a story about the upcoming birth of the baby, which was still a few months off. Their stories, which are reproduced here, remind us once again that children are ready to learn the facts, and though they don't have all of the information correct, they are developing values about family on the basis of the information they do have. The questions at the end of the stories are questions Jeff and Jennifer wanted to research further.

Jennifer (Age 7.2)

1. *The Daddy Has a sprem. And also the daddy has a way of putting a sprem in to the mommy When the baby is ready to come out they go to the hospitle. And the mother whats [waits] pathintle [patiently] for the baby to come out and when the baby is ready to come out they take the mother in the operation room. and the baby comes out close to the mothers vagina. the head comes out first. and if the baby is not ready to come out they half to put it in a machine. and trys to make it as close as posible as they try to make it exzalde like a mothers tummy.*
2. *even when a mother walks through a snowstorm And is hits some thing hard the baby will still be ok. And I forgot this important thing the sprem goes into the mothers uterus and forms the seed into a growing baby.*

3. *how does a mother get a seed at first?* _____

_____

how does a Daddy get a sprem at first? _____

_____

Jeffrey (Age 8.6)

1. *How do people gets babys.*

   *First of all a baby egg comes down in to this certin place.
   I don't rember what it's called. Then the Daddy sticks his
   penis in the mommys vocani like this.*

   *Then abut 2000 sperms go in to the momy. Now I'm sure
   you want to know how the sperms are made. Well you
   know that little sack that hangs from the penis. Well the
   sperms are made in their.*

2. *They go at the egg and one sperm usely hits the egg. After
   that know more sperms can hit the egg and the egg is reday
   to be a child.*

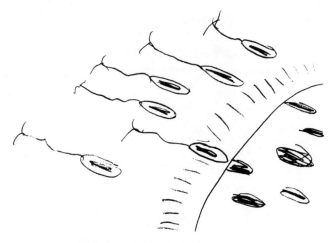

First the egg rolls down into the uterus and plants it self thier. As the days past and turn into mouths and turn into years the baby has to grow in thier for nine mouths.

3. Then the exsiting part happens. The baby is going to be born. First the momy goes to the doctors.

The doctor told the mommy to lie down on a table. And thier they wait till the baby is ready to be born.

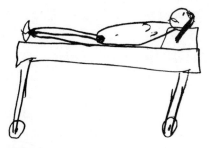

When it is ready to be born, it goes thru the uterus and down into the vacani. The musels stregtchs and stregtchs and stregths even more and the head of the baby pops out.

And then it's body and arms and last of all the feet and legs come out. Then the momy has to stay in the hospital for a little longer. and then she gets to go home whith the baby.

How do the sperms move? _____

_____

How are the sperms made? _____

_____

How does the egg turn into a cild? _____

_____

B. Before puberty, young people should be informed about their sexual response, how it feels, what it's for. The rewarding challenge for parents is to prepare a child for the emotional dimension of sexuality and to communicate effective and constructive moral values. The parent's own emotions and values are all important as a model for the child. Thousands of silent, nonverbal messages in the privacy of the home are sent to every child from birth onward that influence sexual development. If the body is considered good, to be enjoyed, and a channel to communicate personal love and affection, sex is also likely to be seen as personal and loving. When parents are happy with their own sexual feelings, they convey happy feelings to the children.

One mother, Sidney Callahan, has written:

> While retaining their own personal privacy, parents need to let their children know that there are intense emotions involved in sexual experience. If children are equipped only with the biological facts they are still unprepared for their own experience of sex. Young people will also think that their parents must be dense or totally asexual and not part of the real world if the parents never mention the most important sexual phenomenon: i.e., it feels wonderful and people want to continue once they have begun. If a child is not prepared for his or her sexual desire and pleasure, then one of the most important factors has been inexplicably left out of sex education.[14]

C. Create an open and questioning family atmosphere so that new information can be progressively incorporated into your young person's value system. Since questions are answered in terms of the child's age and ability to understand, the answers will contain additional information as the child's understanding expands.

Callahan goes on to explain:

> Sex educators stress the importance of answering questions truthfully. They add, however, that "you don't have to tell the whole truth in intricate detail all at once when a child asks one question . . . also the language used should be appropriate to the child's readiness." In addition to following the child's lead I think parents should do more. Parents have to take the initiative in sex education just as they must in any other aspect of socialization. In my opinion parents should get books from the library and read them to the child early on. All libraries, most schools and some religious education programs will have lists of appropriate books for parents to use. Different books or even specially prepared comic books can be used for children and adolescents at different ages. If parents feel inadequate in their job as sex educators, there are also books to help them. Of course no book is ever going to do the whole job for either parent or child, but it is a start.
>
> One point should be mentioned: if as a parent you find yourself getting particularly hesitant and uncomfortable, it may be a clue to something you should consider. Is there something you haven't worked out in your own sexual development? As usual, education is a two-way enterprise, since to teach is to learn. All parents can better themselves; some must try harder. At any rate whatever correct information is given will be better than the misinformation our supposedly well-educated children will pick up from their peers.[15]

It is comforting to know that most young people come through adolescence without deep emotional scars surrounding their sexual experience. But what about young people with sexual problems? It is helpful for parents to think in terms of a young person's sexual problems and their solutions as reflecting one of three levels.

Level I

Information needs are characteristic of Level I individuals. These young people are not sexually involved to any great degree, and their comments display a lack of accurate information. Their problems are typified in comments such as, "All I know about sex I have learned from my friends"; "I don't know anything about my sexual apparatus; I'm just gonna experiment and find out"; "John and I got really carried away the other night; we were kissing and petting in the car, and I'm wondering if that means I'll get pregnant." These comments show a need for proper information and a value structure for behavior. Many young people need information, and they need it badly, since for many, ignorance is a major contributor to sexual difficulties. Young people in this category are not deeply troubled emotionally, but they need some straightforward and accurate information, or they will be! Information alone, however, is not enough. In addition, they need some direction on how to act toward the other sex. Family members are supposed to provide this modeling, but many families do a poor job.

Level II

Level II individuals are involved sexually and are experiencing emotional difficulty because of this involvement. Their problems are typified by the person who cannot talk to his or her parents, and who will say something like, "If Mom knew what I had done, she would go through the ceiling." Occasionally, this level of problem is evidenced by parents who are anxious because they've never known how to talk to their young person about sex. They may have overheard partial conversations about wild parties which are painful to believe, and they don't quite know how to approach the matter with their son or daughter. These situations usually are indicative of relationship problems that benefit from short-term therapy. The therapist can provide third-party directions for the parents or the young person, giving them some help in how to deal with each other and some encouragement to try to handle the situation themselves.

If there is not a great deal of emotional trauma, and if communication has been good in the past, it is generally preferable that the family work out the problem with little or no intervention by a professional. For any parent or young person who desires counsel, however, it seems valuable to seek outside advice so that they can approach the situation with the feeling that they are proceding in the most skillful way they know.

Level III

The Level III person is involved in a situation that is already deeply emotionally destructive. These difficulties usually require therapeutic intervention. In such highly emotional situations, deterioration has already taken place and depression has been in evidence for sometime. The young person is making impulsive self-destructive decisions and doing things that are not in his/her best interest. For example, one mother came to see me because her daughter was pregnant and the mother was insisting on an abortion. The emotions of both people were raw, and they couldn't talk for more than two or three minutes without blowing up at each other. In another case, a young man at college had begun sleeping with his girlfriend, and he had been experiencing intense guilt because of this relationship. Most of these emotionally confusing situations will be best helped through the aid of an outside person, usually a professional counselor.

Solutions

As indicated, the solution must fit the level of the problem. The first level of ignorance requires solutions that are rational.

Such solutions might be to read the right kind of information; or to offer some friendly suggestions about people to talk to who have an expertise in the relevant area. In short, problem-solving techniques will be useful at this level. Neither the child nor the parent needs additional training or therapy at this point. When the information is provided, and the parent or the young person does what is suggested, wait and see if the problem is solved. I must emphasize, however, that information which is "modeled" is learned best. Thus, visual material—charts, movies, or film strips—along with contact with adults in healthy same-sex and opposite-sex relationships will help the young person make sense out of the new information.

With problems at Level II, there are difficulties between people; for instance, "I want to talk with my son, but I don't know how"; or "I want to talk to Mom and Dad, but how do I begin? How can I get them to listen to me?" When I hear statements like these, it's often an indication that the person needs some ideas, maybe some role playing, some kind of track to get started on. Usually there is no need for much more than short-term intervention from a professional. This can encourage the family and help them know how to do the right thing. In such cases, I will give the parents some tools and some guidelines and encourage them to go to it. When an adolescent comes to me, I will outline some suggestions and possibly role play with them ways they might approach the situation at home, and encourage them to give it a try.

When family relationships are at a stalemate, and there is a great deal of hostility or emotional difficulty, it is a good indication of a Level III problem. When this is the case, it will not be sufficient to give friendly advice or to consider a seminar on human potential training. The situation is past that point. What the individual or family needs is the careful, specific attention of a professional.

NOTES

1. Genesis 16:1–4 (Living Bible).
2. Genesis 26:8 (RSV).
3. Genesis 29:17 (Living Bible).
4. 2 Samuel 11:2–5 (Living Bible).
5. Joshua 2:1 (Living Bible).
6. Lewis B. Smedes, *Sex for Christians* (Grand Rapids, Mich.: William Eerdmans, 1976), p. 76.
7. Smedes, p. 32.
8. Smedes, p. 38.
9. Smedes, p. 39.
10. Taber, C. R. "Sex, Sexual Behavior," *The Interpreters Dictionary of the Bible*, Volume 4, R-Z (Nashville: Abingdon Press, 1962), pp. 296–301.
    Baab, O. J., "Sex, Sexual Behavior," *The Interpreters Dictionary of the Bible*, Supplementary Volume (Nashville: Abingdon Press, 1976), pp. 817–820.
11. A. C. Kinsey, W. B. Pomeroy, and C. E. Martin, *Sexual Behavior in the Human Male* (Philadelphia: Saunders, 1948).
12. W. H. Masters and V. E. Johnson, *Human Sexual Response* (Boston: Little, Brown and Company, 1966).
13. Shere Hite, *The Hite Report*, (Dell Publishing, 1976).
14. Hite, p. 527.
15. Sidney Callahan, "Parents and Sex Education," *Marriage and Family Living*, November 1977, p. 10.
16. Callahan, p. 10.

4. Two Difficult Situations: Masturbation And Abortion

As a psychologist, I have chosen to explore two further situations connected with sexuality. Masturbation, which is known to be extremely common in young boys and girls, is only recently beginning to be discussed openly. Abortion, a far less common but exceedingly more complex dilemma, has been highly debated and publicized.

MASTURBATION

Masturbation, generally defined as self-stimulation of the genitals, is a sexual behavior frequently discussed, often roundly condemned, and universally practiced. Although Charlie Shedd, pastor and author, referred to masturbation in *The Stork Is Dead*, as "God's greatest invention,"[1] there

are other pastors and theologians who would claim that masturbation is the tool of the devil. Thus, it seems fair to say
that masturbation is still clouded by a certain amount of con-
troversy and a lot of emotional concern.

What do we know about masturbation? As Christians, we
must look to the Bible for guidelines for sexual relationships.
We can say that the Bible says nothing directly in reference
to masturbation. In the one text in Genesis (Gen. 38:4–10),
what is referred to as "Onan's sin" is interpreted by most
scholars to be a sin because it is disobedience, not because
it is masturbation. If that is the case, then the Bible is silent
on this sex practice. I suppose it is also safe to say that masturbation was probably practiced in biblical times. It would seem
highly unusual that a practice so prevalent today would be
absent in biblical times, since the Bible speaks frequently of
sexuality and sexual relationships.

There appear to be no negative physical consequences from
practicing masturbation. Some of the earlier fears—developing
warts, growing hair on the palm of your hand, losing your
hair, or going crazy—are now known to be myths that apparently developed in an effort to control the habit of masturbation.

I believe that masturbation can have both positive and negative consequences. Stimulation of the genitals does produce
a powerful pleasure experience leading to and including orgasm. One young man, relating his first orgasm through masturbation, told me: "I was thoroughly amazed that my body
could do such a thing. It was very exciting and pleasurable
and I have no recollection of any negative emotions such as
guilt." I agree with Charlie Shedd that any gift of creation
can also be abused.

"Let's not kid ourselves," writes Shedd. "Many of God's
blessings become cursings when they are not used intelligently.

But like so many other things it is really up to us. . . ."

"So long as masturbation is not humiliating; so long as it helps you to keep on the good side of sociable; so long as you can accept it as a natural part of growing up; then you thank God for it and use it as a blessing".[2]

What are the negative consequences? Though masturbation apparently has no negative physical affect, for some it can leave unresolved psychological conflict that may be extremely traumatic. I will suggest three areas for consideration. These will be followed by some questions I use in determining whether or not this practice has been harmful psychologically.

Masturbation can become obsessive, compulsive, and guilt-producing. The psychological term *obsessive* has to do with a person's thinking. The term *compulsive* has to do with a person's actions. The term *guilt* has to do with a person's violation of a standard of behavior.

Masturbation becomes *obsessive* when the individual becomes preoccupied with sexual thinking or sexual fantasies. These sexual thoughts involve people and situations that are unrealistic and fantasy-oriented. When an individual is obsessed with sexual thinking, most of the waking hours are spent daydreaming and imagining sexual involvement far beyond what is realistic.

Predictably, the individual withdraws into this fantasy life. He or she becomes more and more isolated from family and friends, developing the lifestyle of a "loner." It is not uncommon to hear parents say: "Bob is spending more and more time in his room lately." "Sally doesn't spend any time with her friends; she seems to be content to be by herself." "Phil seems to be somewhere else most of the time." "Every once in a while Debbie talks about Steve, her new boyfriend; but I've never seen him, and she's never had a date with him."

Obsessive behavior built around masturbation and sexual fantasies is destructive psychologically because it nudges an individual further and further from reality, until truth itself is a stranger to the person. Friends begin to catch on to the delusion. Though they sometimes play along with it for a while, they soon recognize the behavior as troubled and either withdraw from the individual or encourage their friend to get some professional help.

Compulsive behavior has to do with an individual's actions. We refer to compulsive behaviors as habits. Thus, if an individual compulsively masturbates, he or she masturbates more and more often as times goes on. Often there is a certain amount of ritual connected with the practice. Individuals discovering their sexual potency through masturbation sometimes find themselves masturbating two, three, four, or ten times a day. This habit is sometimes connected with pornographic literature, articles of clothing, or sexual fantasies. In addition, some individuals obtain gratification from the challenge of masturbating in risky situations, for example, public restrooms or other places where getting caught is possible.

The destructive psychological consequences of compulsive masturbation are similar to those of obsessive masturbation. An individual becomes very egocentric, very much tuned into self-gratification, and often displays isolated and withdrawn behavior.

The third area of psychological difficulty is that masturbation can be extremely *guilt-producing*. Psychologists have made us aware that there are two types of guilt—true guilt and false guilt. The Bible talks about guilt in Romans 7:14. It seems that God has given us a conscience "written on our hearts" to help keep us on the beam. The purpose of this conscience is to alert us when we have dealt inappropriately with ourselves, others, the universe, and God. Thus, we must examine scripture to help identify the type of behavior we should feel guilty for—true guilt.

We also learn from the behavioral sciences that we develop

a conscience through learning. As we grow up, our parents and other significant people help us develop a sense of right and wrong, often referred to as our *value system*. When we violate this sense of right and wrong, which is well established by age 6, we feel guilty; in other words, we become anxious and nervous and feel a certain amount of worthlessness. Some of the things we feel guilty about, however, should probably be put into the category of false guilt. That is, there are really no good reasons from scripture or from our knowledge of human behavior to feel anxious and nervous about these behaviors. Some sources of false guilt would be having sexual feelings, being angry occasionally, missing school or work when we are sick, or stating our firm beliefs when they differ from those of others. The task of an individual moving toward maturity is to be in touch with guilt feelings so that he or she can "stay on the beam." True guilt should be listened to carefully and followed, while we should go to work to defeat the feelings identified as false guilt. These feelings are often well ingrained from our childhood and take a great deal of work to change.

What can we now say briefly about masturbation and its development? Infancy is the time to lay the foundation for people's acceptance of their body. Infants need to be held and touched, along with hearing words of endearment. In this way, they learn early that their body—every part of it— is OK. Natural opportunities such as holding, nursing, bathing, and dressing an infant provide situations for communicating this "OK-ness." Infants are not fragile; they need to be handled, and it is this handling and touching that helps develop a positive sexuality.

Elimination for the infant is also a time of developing feelings for sexuality. Elimination is natural to the infant. It is not "dirty" or in any way repulsive. If, however, the parent associates changing diapers with a time of disgust, the infant may begin to pick up some messages that his or her genitals are dirty or disgusting. To the parent, changing diapers should be natural, matter-of-fact, and conducted with the same sensitivity and warmth that is communicated at other times. In addition, I would encourage fathers to participate fully in this activity.

At some time during the first year, your infant will probably discover his or her genitals. Our son Jason, who was not yet six months, had just found his feet. He was absolutely enthralled with his feet; as far as he knew, they were a new toy, fun to play with. Soon he realized they were connected to his body, and he derived even more pleasure from doing things with his feet. His feet, however, will not be as pleasurable as his genitals. Genitals are naturally and especially pleasurable. God made them that way. Jason will probably fondle his genitals, and maybe he will fondle them more than he plays with his feet. This is natural. Little boys soon discover their penis, and little girls discover their clitoris. This natural source of pleasure will be fondled occasionally because it is enjoyable.

Very few children actually masturbate. Masturbation is usually an interpretation of parents who overreact, panic, and rush to the nearest psychologist for fear that their child will become perverted. Children who seem to fondle their genitals frequently are often giving parents a clue that they need more affection. Parents should not call attention to the fondling by demanding, "Stop that!" or by slapping the child's hands. Rather, the parent should pick up the child, responding to the fondling as a sign of the need for more affection. Any excessive fondling will quite likely soon disappear. Where children continue excessive fondling, parents are wise to seek the advise of a competent professional.

Current statistics[3] indicate that a high percentage (95%)

of young males, and an increasingly high percentage (70%) of young females, masturbate. In fact, young men usually discover their sexual potency through masturbation. This is not true with young females to the degree that it is with young males. Studies do reveal that most young people, at one time or another during their adolescence, masturbate, some to orgasm and some not to orgasm. This is certainly a behavior that can be talked about as parents seek to prepare their young person for sexual responsiveness. It can be presented in a way that will minimize the negative consequences and help the young person develop a healthy approach to his or her own sexuality. For example, the book *Preparing for Adolescence*[4] may be helpful for you to read together, especially the chapter "Something Crazy Is Happening to My Body." This is by Dr. James Dobson, professor of pediatrics and popular speaker and author.

In summary, a young person needs to realize that while the Bible says nothing directly about masturbation, and while there are no destructive physical consequences, there can be some rather traumatic psychological effects in that masturbation can become obsessive or compulsive. It should be mentioned also that masturbation is a "single-sex" activity, and engaging in it to excess may make it more difficult to adjust in a heterosexual relationship. The young person, however, should not feel excessive guilt over masturbation, and hopefully will have developed at least one trusting adult relationship with a person who will help locate professional assistance if masturbation is indeed a problem.

The questions I ask young people who talk to me about masturbation are these:

- How does it leave you feeling about yourself and your relationship to others?

- Is it controlling you?
- Does it cause lust (a preoccupation with the sexual aspect of relationships)?

With these thoughts as lead-in, I take a counseling approach and say, "Let's talk about it."

I've come to the personal conclusion that, for the young single person, for the divorced or widowed individual, and in a marriage relationship, masturbation is a sexual alternative; however, the psychological consequences must be considered. It is important for us to remember that the Bible has a high view of sexuality as part of a relationship, and if it detracts from the wholeness of that relationship, it must be approached with a certain amount of caution. Masturbation, as single sex, could potentially detract from relationships.

ABORTION

The question of abortion comes up in many different situations. A 40-year-old wealthy wife and mother becomes pregnant while having an affair with a prominent local citizen. She leaves town, has an abortion, and is back in three days. A 15-year-old waits four months to share the fact that she has had an abortion. A high school senior in a panic tells her mother she's pregnant, but her military boyfriend is anxious and willing to marry her. Her mother nevertheless insists on an abortion. A single career woman arranges for an abortion after discovering that she is pregnant. She goes on a vacation, comes back suntanned but shaken. A young couple is not interested in children. The wife becomes pregnant, and they arrange for an abortion.

In my own work with young people and their families, I have come to two conclusions that I hold in tension as I counsel people seeking to deal with this dilemma. The first conclusion is that I am against abortion on demand for reasons other than incest, rape, or danger to the mother. My reasons are not psychological and practical, but primarily spiritual: It goes against my view of God's intended design for life to abort a fetus. Though this view is deep within me, my heart of compassion knows the importance of taking each case under careful consideration.

A second conclusion I have come to is that our communities have very few support systems to help a young person facing the abortion question. By the time the young woman gets to me, she has usually been rejected and ostracized, and the potential for humiliation hangs over her head, if it has not already been realized. She usually has no place to turn for the support needed to carry the child. Thus, though I have a very high view of life after conception, I realize that the future facing a pregnant young woman can be uncertain and dismal, making the decision extremely difficult. I can understand why medical people take both sides of the issue. I can also understand why women and theologians stand on both sides of the issue.

I will limit my remarks here to teenage pregnancies, attempting to provide guidelines for parents and young women who find themselves facing this dilemma. In my counseling with parents and young women, there are two situations most often encountered: (1) the young woman who has already had an abortion and is sharing the information with her parents, and (2) the young woman who has recently discovered she is pregnant and is asking her parents for help in making a decision about the pregnancy.

First, there can be serious emotional consequences as a result of an abortion, but this does not happen in all cases. Abortion seems to be like many other emotionally loaded situations: it can be a learning experience or an emotionally devastating one. Secondly, young women who carry the fetus through to birth can suffer as many, if not more, destructive emotional consequences. Third, there are critical factors that affect either decision, including the personalities of the pregnant women and of those significant others who help her make her decision. Equally as important are the resources available to her to implement her decision.

Some resources that I have found indispensable in making it possible for a pregnant young woman to face her situation are: (1) a home where the girl will feel cared for as an individual; (2) practical help in dealing with the situation constructively; and (3) a resource center—maybe a church—where prenatal care and counseling can be found.

My wish for women facing this decision is a chance to work through the decision carefully with the help of those who are wise and compassionate. If the parents and the young woman are preoccupied with family status and embarrassment, the decision is likely to have an effect similiar to that of alcohol on the alcoholic: it is simply an escape from the pressure of a problem. The decision is likely to have much more positive effects if people are concerned about owning up to the difficult questions: What choices did I make to get into this? What does this say about my approach to life? How will the family support an individual who needs additional resources over the next few months? By facing these questions and by allowing others to face them with you, you have a much greater chance for positive growth and development in the lives of all those who are involved.

Any parents confronted by their young daughter who either is pregnant or who has just had an abortion are suddenly aware that there are issues that make each situation different. Let's consider some.

If you are a Christian and believe that life goes on after death, you will look at the question differently than if your approach to life is to squeeze all you can out of this temporal existence because "that's all there is." Also, if your own happiness is your highest priority, you may make a different decision than if you highly value the importance of others. Third, if pregnancy resulted from rape, you may decide differently than if pregnancy resulted from a willing sexual act, even though pregnancy was not your objective.

The challenge for the parent is to make a good decision based on as much information as possible. Explore, explore, explore.

My own conviction is that decisions involving abortion are usually in a category of a tragic moral choice. Any decision will probably have both advantages and disadvantages, and must be weighed carefully. These are some of the realities facing women who consider abortion:

- Women are having abortions; it is legal.
- Many young potential mothers are facing difficult emotional and "impossible" economic futures. They probably are "unfit" mothers.
- In our society, men bear little, if any, responsibility during the pregnancy and for support following birth.
- Some women carrying a child face difficult social stigmas, as do many of their families.
- There are very few support services for an unmarried young woman who carries her child to term and who needs resources.

These situations and others are reasons given for terminating pregnancy with abortion. I have sat for hours discussing each of them in order to arrive at a conclusion. One question is definitely a spiritual issue—what does each person believe about life for the fetus and the woman.

Some individuals claim that if an individual has no particular religious convictions but lives within a framework of humanism, there will probably be few psychological after-effects if a responsible decision has been worked through. Though this view looks reasonable, I am continually amazed at the unresolved guilt carried for years by some women who have had abortions. It appears that humanism does not offer the complete answer to this problem.

Individuals who believe in eternal life and have a high view of life as created by God will have to consider their responsibility in light of these convictions. Not all Christians will agree; some have abortions while others do not, both on strong personal convictions. And some in each of these groups make the wrong decision.

Christians must consider such Scripture passages as Luke 1:15; Jeremiah 1:4,5; Genesis 25:21–23; Matthew 1:18; and Psalms 139:13–16—all of which indicate that God has a plan for a person's life while the person is yet unborn. These Scriptures, along with the Bible's high view of life, make abortion a difficult decision that has to be weighed carefully.

The important questions to be considered are:

- What was the situation surrounding conception?
- Is there danger to the mother or child?
- Are there support systems available to provide for both the mother and the child during the time of pregnancy and following birth?

This third question is important and in some ways an indictment on the church, which, incidentally, is you and me, not the building on the corner. Women young and old have experienced rejection and desertion at times when they need support from Christian friends or the church. For many, abortion is the only way to avoid unbearable consequences.

Recently at the Dale House, two babies have been born and put up for adoption. This was the choice made by the women involved. Their decision to carry the babies received the support of some in the community while others opposed it, but once the decision was made, all of us pitched in and supported the people involved. I am convinced this can be a constructive situation when people are working together. We also have experienced a number of abortions in the community. There are no data available on which resolution has been best. Serious consideration has been given in each case by professionals, parents, the young woman herself, and her friends. I am convinced that each situation needs our best efforts.

NOTES

1. Charlie W. Shedd, *The Stork Is Dead* (Waco, Tex.: Word, 1968), pp. 70–73.
2. Shedd, p. 73.
3. McCary, James Leslie, *Human Sexuality*, 2nd Edition (Florence, Ken.: D. Van-Nostrand Company, 1973), pg. 156.
4. James Dobson, *Preparing for Adolescence* (Santa Ana, Calif.: Vision House Publishers, 1978), pp. 67–90.

5. Social Change

Earl Nightingale, radio commentator, tells the story of an angry father shouting "Why don't you grow up?" at his 12-year-old son. The sudden silence in the room as the boy struggled to control his tears was finally broken by, "That's what I'm trying to do!"[1]

Isn't that what all young people are trying to do? Growing up is not an easy job.

PEER INFLUENCE: POWERFUL AGENT OF CHANGE

The second major shift for the young person and the family is a social one. Social changes are not altogether new, and it's good to remember that. I remember my son Jeff at age 4, wanting a football shirt, "like Peter" next door. Even at that age, this social shift was evident. It begins early and occurs consistently through the years; however, during adolescence it creates a much more intense atmosphere. It will help us as parents to remember that even as adults we have to deal with intense social pressure, and we've been trying to get along well with people for years! For the young person, the social setting becomes a major, and often competitive, learning climate—a fertile ground for growth.

Nightingale takes off from the story about the father and son by observing:

> If someone talked to us that way, "Why don't you grow up?" we'd punch him in the nose, but a youngster can't punch his parents in the nose, much as he'd love to, so the fire just builds within him. He reacts to the parent who treats him in this manner just exactly as you or I would—he hates him. He doesn't want to. He's terribly disappointed in the parent and in himself. He's torn by the wish to love, the need to love and the hate he feels. This is the kind of tumultuous inner battle that an adult finds most difficult to handle and resolve. In a child, or a very young person, when everything in life looms so much bigger, so much more final, more terrible, it takes on catastrophic proportions.
>
> Later, when the young person has grown into adulthood and, hopefully, some degree of maturity, he and his parent, or parents, may become friends again. He may even make exactly the same mistakes with his kids.
>
> But it's a costly shame that we look upon our children, so often, differently from the way we look at other people. And not all parents do. Some parents treat their youngsters with courtesy, respect and love, and at the same time lay down firm guidelines and rules of conduct.[2]

One father who has been in and out of all kinds of scrapes with two teenaged sons and a daughter has remarked, "We use the 'discipleship' concept of discipline—which means deciding on the boundaries ahead of time, and making those boundaries tight enough to give direction we both understand, but loose enough so they can move within the boundaries."

As your young person moves toward independence, the peer group exerts more and more influence. Our educational system is structured in such a way that young people spend a great deal of their day together. These peer relationships provide the ingredients for both healthy and unhealthy growth. If there has not been healthy nurturing between birth and 10 years (in areas such as feeling loved and cared for, developing basic skills in relating to other people, a healthy curiosity in understanding the world), the young boy and girl can arrive at adolescence ill-equipped to cope with the kind of stresses they will encounter. The following story shows that though peer relationships are urgently needed at this time, they do not take the place of a good sound family influence.

As a young child, Dan experienced a great deal of rejection from a mother and father who did not like each other. They saw him as one of the few reasons they had stayed together. Both Mom and Dad were alcoholics and did a poor job of parenting Dan during the years when it was important for him to acquire the basic skills of living. Since he was blamed for their staying together, they constantly treated him as a problem and he felt inadequate and worthless; and since his parents treated him as an object to be played with and not a person to be nurtured, he was turned on to drugs and alcohol at about age 4 or 5.

It is not difficult to understand why, at age 11, Dan had two major ways of reacting to the world around him. One was depression, consisting of heavy feelings of hopelessness and worthlessness. The second was withdrawal from all social situations into isolation. As Dan approached adolescence, he banded together with other peers whose common bond was their lack of belonging to anyone. He took his cues from them. Their activities were geared toward instant gratification, which involved drug abuse, vandalism, stealing, and fighting.

Psychological testing showed that although he was flunking out of school, Dan had an average intelligence. In addition, it was found that he resorted to his two defensive strategies—depression and withdrawal—whenever he encountered a difficult situation. He had become emotionally attached to a girlfriend, partly because his emotional needs were unmet at home. So it was not surprising that he cut his wrists when the relationship with the girlfriend was threatened by his parents.

Dan had no foundation of healthy family relationships on which to build his peer relations. Rather, he attempted to fill his emotional void by deriving all his satisfaction from his peers. This was obviously too much to expect; no peers can make up for years of emotional deprivation, when such basic needs as belonging to parents who care and love, and gaining some of the skills needed to manage life, are absent. The damage was too great and had been going on for too long.

Desperately, Dan grabbed and held on to a few peer relationships. When these were threatened, he had nothing to live for. The hurt and rejection over the years had accumulated, and his only means for defending himself was to take his own life. Though he tried to take his life he failed, and he wound up in a hospital.

Dan is an extreme case. Most young people will not fall at this end of the spectrum. However, it points out clearly that while peer relations for a young person have a very critical place in continuing growth and development, they can not take the place of family.

Another illustration of the importance of the social shift is the story of Helen, a plain girl of 14, who is a classic example of the old term *wallflower*. Helen is very quiet, unassuming in her posture, simple in her dress. You almost have to look for Helen to see her; she almost encourages you to pass her by. Peers are a threat to Helen, and she has devised all sorts of strategies to avoid them. Her school activities are limited to nonrelational activities. Her acquaintances would describe her as a loner, someone they feel sorry for, but someone who puts them off as friends. Helen has not been rejected by her parents as Dan has; she has been overly protected so that she has developed no skills in relating to others. She is a lonely girl because no one has taught her how to relate to others in a healthy way. Her major strategy for dealing with life is to avoid it, and then to overcompensate in areas that do not demand anything of her relationally, such as good grades and practicing hours on the recorder, which she plays with her father. Even her dress, grooming, and posture loudly proclaim that she desperately does not want to call attention to herself. Her very being says, "Please leave me alone."

Helen will not be able to benefit from her peers as most young people will. She will go through her adolescence escaping relationships. More than likely, she will arrive at adulthood a lonely, frightened woman with few skills for moving into life in meaningful, fulfilling ways. Helen is another example of a young person who does not develop socially during adolescence because of poor parenting in her early years.

Early adolescence is a time for parents to recognize the importance of peer relationships and to encourage them in constructive ways. Your home belongs to your children as well as to you. Open it up to their friends. Be present to them whenever you can. Provide an atmosphere where healthy discussion and dialogue can take place. Initiate it. Share your own enthusiasms. And in the process of welcoming your children's friends, you will be amazed how much you get out of it too.

It's all too common these days for parents to abdicate their responsibility—to leave the house or to retire behind closed doors and never be seen when kids are around. Be present, but not overbearing. Be visible and watchful, but not obnoxious. Some kids are scared to death if you're not visibly available and quietly caring about what's going on.

A Southern California girl who answered a questionnaire in *Young Life Magazine* says, "I love partying because I'm with the people I want to be with and I'm having fun. But I don't enjoy parties because sometimes I get in trouble." A little older girl from Oregon explains, "Partying lets you have fun with others, but *only* if there is NO drugs or alcohol or cigarettes around. Mostly parties are just to get drunk or get high." A mid-adolescent from Oklahoma says, "I love being with friends, but I don't enjoy parties where people get drunk and act like fools." And a 15-year-old Arkansas boy says, "My idea of fun is doing simple things with good friends. I don't enjoy parties because of beer and drugs."[3]

It is essential for parents to realize the importance of young people learning from each other, of forming real friendships that may not be just passing fancies, as these peer experiences pave the way to future growth and social development. But it is equally urgent that parents be parents and provide a framework of sensible protection.

FRIENDSHIP: A DESPERATE NEED FOR YOUTH

According to Robert Brain, "Ethologists are showing that we come into the world programmed to need love . . . in fact, the need for affection, intimacy, and cooperation may well be instinctive in human beings. . . ."[4]

I suppose it is this need for love that makes us so responsive to others early in life. Our new baby, Jason, just can't get enough loving. He responds to every touch or gentle glance his way. He is even requesting more and more to be held and played with. His socialization will continue to happen at home, but soon, like the older children, he will seek the companionship of other children outside our family.

When their children are very young, parents carefully plan

so that the children can be part of different groups that open the way to new friendships. Some of these groups are part of our culture—birthday parties, church suppers, neighborhood sports, park and recreation classes, school. Parents cannot totally depend on these structures, however; they must seek to discover or construct a group that will meet the needs of their particular child, such as inviting certain children or their families to participate with the family, encouraging or even expressly persuading the child to attend certain functions or to join certain groups, with the assurance that "if it doesn't work out, we'll drop it."

Out of such group activities, friends are chosen. Friendship has been defined as "an intense relationship between two individuals."[5] We are told that children move toward friendships rather naturally, but somewhere during growth and development, we as parents feel we have to restrict their natural tendencies. Our culture seems to have lost the value of this relationship that is so highly prized by other cultures. For any number of reasons, America offers little evidence of the kind of ritual or emotional investment found in the friendship relationship of other cultures.

Can anything be said to help parents encourage the natural tendency toward friendship that is evident during childhood years? Yes. Here are a few suggestions.

- Encourage boys and girls playing together in childhood, even at the early stage (6–9 years old) when frequently boys "don't like girls" and vice versa.
- Encourage the development of friendships through such actions as inviting children's potential friends to spend time in your home, taking potential friends on family outings or vacations, and providing time for the two "buddies" to play and explore together.

- Allow your children to be a part of other families. This provides a place for them to be on their own and "try out" those relationship skills that are being developed.
- Encourage reading about the adventures of friends. Books are powerful teachers, opening doors of excitement unavailable to many of us in our own situations. Of course, young people can escape through books that are not very healthy. Most young people who read, however, greatly enhance the quality of their lives.
- As a child approaches puberty, it is wise to explain thoroughly the sexual responsiveness of both sexes, including the importance of the emotional investment accompanying such a biological change.
- Plan for your child to be part of a structured group, such as a camp, where a counselor will help promote healthy socialization, including some of the ingredients of friendships. We must help raise each other's children, especially during adolescence. This is a time for good adult models to have a significant effect on the life of the adolescent. In America we call it hero identification or hero worship. It can be a positive learning experience, especially when a personal relationship is involved; or it can be destructive, as witnessed by the thousands of young adolescents who mimic the lifestyles, language, and dress of "teen idols." Unfortunately, money has created many of these popular puppets who act out the frustrations of all of us, and who frequently end in heavy drug involvement or violence.

  Thus, we know that modeling is important to this age and we are reminded to select our models carefully. A reality-based experience with a real person can have a significant positive effect on a young person.
- Spend time alone with your son or daughter, allowing for time to talk over how friendships are going: How

does it feel to be left out? Who do you feel is your "best friend?" Would you like to plan something soon with someone special? Discuss what would be fun.

These suggestions may sound too simple or second-nature to many. *Why* then are so many adolescents lonely, selfish, rejected, afraid to be known, and friendless? One mother of a now 25-year-old depressed graduate student confided in me recently, "He has never had a friend in his life." What a tragic commentary! He is going through life using every attention-getting device he can muster—sympathy, pleas, joining groups, self-pity, psychosomatic complaints—and all of these only drive potential friends away. He is miserable.

Encourage your child to have friends and to be a friend. But what can be said for the 11- to 19-year-old tottering on the brink of friendlessness, or five years into a life of loneliness, ego-centeredness, or isolation? If Robert Brain is correct that the need for affection is instinctive, then some form of friendship is imperative for the adolescent.

The biological change discussed in the previous chapter will challenge the young person socially. Interestingly enough, Brain states that "Sexuality is never one of the essential bonds of friendship and can even be an obstacle."[6] Thus, same-sex and opposite-sex friendships are probably desirable and should be encouraged, rather than avoided for fear of destructive sexual involvement. If, in fact, a real friendship is developing, many of the exploitive adolescent social practices, such as the teenage party, will be discarded.

THE PARTY

New urges to socialize will bring young people into contact with others outside the family who will influence their lives. A culture has developed in response to these social needs of young people, a culture that presents both opportunities for social change and intense pressure to conform. One major social event for many young people today is the party.

Usually nothing exciting is planned or expected in the way of activities. The main objective is to be together. Even though they may not particularly like what's happening, young people will make a strong effort to go wherever the party is based. Why? Because the social shift begs for new friends, for people to talk to, for experiments in getting to know each other. In many places the party is the ground for this to take place during adolescence.

The party can also be a very confusing, disturbing event. Often it is an opportunity to experiment freely with liquor and drugs, and sometimes with sex. Teenagers who say they enjoy parties because that's where the people are, may go on to add, "But I don't enjoy seeing my friends drunk or stoned," or "I don't like it when things get out of hand."[7]

An invitation to a party can define those who are "in" and those who are "out" of high school society. Many parties promote sex as a temporary anesthetic against loneliness, drugs and alcohol as a temporary "trip" away from the mundane demands of life, and the false relationship as acceptance based on self-gratification. Unfortunately, for many young people a party is their chance to learn what they have failed to learn at home. The results are often an increasing narcissism and insensitivity, rather than a growth toward wholeness.

Parties are not inherently destructive. A well planned, creative event with some thought for those in attendance, and some understanding supervision, can be provided.

Suggestions for parents:

- Coed group events provide a setting to work on friendships—school, church, community clubs. Most adolescents need such a setting where they can develop relationships. I'm not speaking here only of the shy and withdrawn young person. The school stud has his "crowd"; drug users congregate in the park; the "popular" person needs a stage; and all other less stereotyped ordinary young people need a place; where they can learn to relate. Thus, some kind of setting is essential, even though what may be found is destructive.

- Some informative group or class—probably coed—will help begin to clarify the biological differences between the sexes, especially for young adolescents (11–13).
- Help the young person make friends with a wide range of people. For example, plan activities with your children where they will become familiar with different kinds of involvement and where they will meet new people.
- Initiate and challenge creativity in planning events such as parties. Place emphasis on important life values rather than on selfish pursuits.
- Encourage your young person to explore different areas of personal interest. Initiate times for this to take place and be a participant. The benefits to both of you will be exciting.
- Plan family projects related to the individual interests of each family member. In this way you will help each other grow. Each family member contains a wealth of desires, wishes, and motivation just waiting to be tapped and encouraged. Help some of this get loose and watch the entire family grow.
- Encourage individuals to explore new areas to broaden their interests. Though you might encounter resistance at first, these new risks can provide a setting for new confidence and learning.

The years between 11 and 19 are a prime time for developing social and relationship skills, and parents are important to this development. So often parents feel that the pressure is finally off, and they can now get on with their own lives. This attitude is unfortunate and ill-timed. Families need to continue to operate as families, encouraging each member to develop fully. For the adolescent, it is a time to become more independent and to make social choices that will have an ongoing effect into adulthood. The social settings provided by the adolescent culture, however, are not automatically constructive and healthy, and most young people need their parents to help them make good choices that will provide meaningful growth experiences.

NOTES

1. Earl Nightingale, "That's What They're Trying To Do," *Success Unlimited,* April 1978, p. 16.
2. Nightingale, p. 16.
3. Statements quoted are from answers to questionnaire: "Who Am I Anyway?" *Young Life Magazine,* Spring 1978, pp. 8–10.
4. Robert Brain, "Someone Else Should Be Your Own Best Friend," *Psychology Today,* October 1977, p. 123.
5. Brain, p. 120.
6. Brain, p. 120.
7. "Who Am I Anyway?" *Young Life Magazine,* Spring 1978.

6. Intellectual Change

A third major shift for the young adolescent is a shift in thinking ability. This new capacity will affect all areas of life, including parent-child interaction and family structure. It will influence the development of personality characteristics; defense mechanisms; future goals; concerns for social, religious, and political values; and personal identity. In fact, some experts say that this change has the most important long-lasting effect of any of the three shifts discussed here. Though this fact may first appear to be obvious, it is frequently discounted or overlooked by adults who fail to recognize its significance. There seems to be widespread agreement that this new ability and desire to think and to reason has profound implications for both personal and family life. It becomes very important now in the family situation that a young person be allowed to think through a situation, and be held responsible for the consequences of his or her choices, all the while being supported by interested parents.

A NEW TYPE OF CAPABILITY

What this means is that the parents (or people in authority) no longer have to sit down and lead the young person through each step to make sure the right answer is found. The thinking apparatus of most young people is now capable of following a situation to its conclusion and making a decision to act on the basis of that mental process. That's not to say that young people won't make mistakes, and that these mistakes won't be very costly. But the family is the proper place to make those mistakes, to try and to fail. Then young people can figure out with you what went wrong and how to make a better choice next time. My point is that a young person is now ready to exercise judgment, and must be allowed to use and develop that responsibility and learn how to exert that power *in the family.*

Because Mark is now 13, he has not suddenly been infused with the ability to make good judgments. If Mark's parents have not taught him, somewhere between the ages of 3 and 12, to recognize various alternatives and to make appropriate choices, they can hardly expect him to suddenly possess that skill. Again we are faced with the fact that skills are accrued as interest on capital, a day at a time. Thus, even though Mark has acquired new thinking skills due to the normal growth process, he will not be able to use them effectively unless he has daily practice.

In another family, Bob was always told what to do and when to do it. His parents thought they had his best interest in mind. Bob was obedient—a "nice kid"—but at about age 14 he began feeling some peer pressure. It didn't seem to be anything serious; it was related primarily to dress and school functions. Certain styles were "in," and Bob knew it. Also, it was "good" to be seen at certain functions. Most of his requests in these area were met with negative comments from his parents. He had never experienced conflict with his parents before, at least not any that mattered much. He had no model for, or training in, how to approach a disagreement, so he pushed it inside himself and there it simmered.

His parents had few clues that he was accumulating this anger. They thought he was going through a withdrawal stage, and that he would soon outgrow it and realize that they had his best interest in mind.

Bob began to lie to avoid disagreements. He would tell his parents he was going one place when he was actually going somewhere else. He had a friend keep some clothes for him that he could change into on special occasions. But, as is usually the case, Bob's parents got wind of his doings and confronted him. Again, Bob had no previous model for dealing with confrontation. He had lied, he knew it. He felt exposed, small, and naughty. When he was a little child, his mother would slap his hands and tell him "Big boys don't do those things!" Now he was big, still doing "those things" and feeling the same feelings he had felt then.

His mind searched wildly for a reason, an excuse, anything to convince them he had not been disobedient. "I met some kids and they talked me into going"; "a friend picked me up in his car and took me there"; "I got lost"—anything that might sound legitimate. Sometimes it worked, and sometimes it didn't. When it didn't, Bob never gave in, even when the evidence was obvious. To admit that he was disobedient was to violate the highest standard in the family, and he just could not face that.

Often he could outwit his parents. He had matured in his thinking enough to strategize. When he was younger he always got caught, but not any more. His strategies were becoming more and more sophisticated, and most of the time he was "winning."

Though Bob had not learned how to face his problems, his thinking capacity had increased. He no longer had to experience each situation to figure out what would happen. He could think about it and plan his strategy carefully. He had an idea, however, that at some point in the future he and his parents were going to have to "have it out." There were just too many lies in the air.

Like all children, Bob dealt with conflict, but the methods he had learned were destructive. He learned to "keep your thoughts to yourself" and to "do what you want to do even if others disagree, only don't get caught." Slowly the attitude "if you don't get caught, its ok" developed and became a way of life.

Bob's parents should have started early to teach him to face conflicts, to discuss alternative solutions, and to come to a mutual decision with him. With young children, the parent provides a great deal of guidance in choosing the path to follow. And as the child becomes older, the parent takes a "let's try it and see what happens" attitude. The child learns with experience what the consequences are and how they can be avoided next time. The place where parents need to draw the line, however, is where there is too much risk of physical or emotional danger involved. Sometimes parents just need to say "No!" As we will discuss later, research indicates that young people benefit the most from a family run in a democratic manner where the parents have ultimate authority. Neither a rigid enforcement of set rules that have always existed in the family, nor a "do as you please" form of family government seem to "pull the freight."

Bob and his parents may be headed for some counseling

to help the family develop a style of operation that allows each member to grow. Bob is no longer 8 years old, and it is high time that he is encouraged to make some of his own choices and to experience the consequences of those choices with his parents' support.

Up to now Bob has been choosing and forcing the consequences. However, there has been no communication, understanding or agreement with his parents. Lying, secrecy, and snooping has been the "order of the day" and these patterns of relating are hurtful and dishonest. When things have gone this far it is often necessary to "get it all out on the table," "sift through the pieces," and begin to put the puzzle back together carefully. Chapter 8 "Guidelines For Growth and Understanding" gives some direction for this.

Another family came for counseling because of their daughter, Karen, 16, who had no intention of letting her parents run her life. They were supposed to provide her with good clothing and shelter, and she would take care of the rest. The family could do what they wanted, but they were to stay out of her business. Karen's mother had felt a great deal of guilt over how she had raised her first two children and was not going to make the same mistake with Karen. Karen learned early that the way to get her way was to make Mom feel guilty. So she did: "You never made John do this"; "You bought Amy more than you buy me"; and the ultimate guilt producer, "If you don't, I'll kill myself!" usually got Karen exactly what she wanted.

As Karen approached adolescence, her thinking capacity changed. She now was able to think through her approach of how to get what she wanted. Her strategies became refined, always hitting Mom's "tender spots," always one step ahead of Mom's counterattack. Just when Mom thought she would never let that happen again, Karen let loose with another, well-oiled, well-thought-through plan. Everything—from playing sick, to a hostile barrage of vile language, to minor attempts at suicide with lots of warning and "you'll be sorry" messages—was attempted. Mom was, shall we say, "up against the wall."

Karen, like Bob, had not learned to face life and be responsible for her actions. She had learned, rather, that the world owed her a living, and she was going to squeeze it for every drop she could get. She was miserable, and her new thinking capacity only made living responsibly even more difficult. At age 16, her lifestyle is well defined, and change may have to come with a great deal of difficulty and pain for both Karen and her parents.

NEW THINKING AND ITS CONSEQUENCES

This new capacity for thinking Jean Piaget, the developmental psychologist, calls the stage of *formal operations*.[1] It is usually identified as existing from age 12 on. Young people now have a general inclination to solve problems. They are able to consider possible options as to how a problem might be solved. I encourage parents to take time to sit down and help their young person "sort through" various solutions and their possible consequences. I assure you, this will be time well spent, and it will most likely pay rich dividends in the future.

Because this is a time of rapid body changes and new social pressures, these subjects will need to be considered. Young people will wonder, What is happening to my body and what effect will that have on my relationships with girls, with boys, and on my thoughts about myself? What kind of friendships should I seek to establish, and what are the possible consequences of these friendships? How can I use my abilities to think to my best advantage?

Another consequence of this new thinking ability is a tendency toward self-awareness, along with a sensitivity, even an oversensitivity, to rejection. Long periods of time can be spent thinking about what one is like and how one affects others. This can result in a hypersensitivity and an unrealistic view of oneself, or it can result in a realistic appraisal of oneself, one's abilities, and how to use them most effectively for growth. This tendency for self-reflection provides a natural setting for parents to listen and to help the young person sort out feelings and facts.

Early adolescence can be a discouraging and frustrating time for parents attempting to help a young person overwhelmed with feelings of rejection. It seems that the very gift of new thinking abilities can turn against a young person who is already overwhelmed by feelings of rejection, intensifying those feelings as he or she so easily misinterprets the responses of others. Such feelings can result in depression, and the person may need professional attention if the depression persists. It takes a sensitive, patient parent who can "hang in there" and be a friend during these times of self-doubt, a parent who can deal with his or her own pain and still provide support at the right time. For most young people, the change is exciting, moving them toward the possibility of independence—"Maybe I can make my own decisions." Parents can provide a challenge for these young people, helping them ask hard questions and posing creative solutions to seemingly impossible problems. They also can enter into preparing for an exam, selecting a college, applying for a job, working out a conflict, or developing the skills of conversation, by providing new insights, suggestions, advice, or other types of support.

As a general rule, parents want to help their children develop the ability to learn from the past, live in the present, and move toward the future. Help now will minimize making the same mistake over and over, and maximize making good judgments now; it will also open a more effective approach to the future with plans that are realistic. Parents of 12- and 13-year-olds find themselves providing lots of advice and direction; parents of 15- and 16-year-olds become partners in solutions; and from then on, if things have gone well, they only lend a hand when asked.

Though I could write a hundred case studies, detailing different dynamics for each one, you really need to write your own. The guidelines I have suggested are rather general and must be adapted to each situation with a great deal of sensitivity and understanding.

Here are some roadblocks that can hamper positive adolescent growth:

- During childhood, problem-solving techniques have been neither taught nor encouraged.
- As the child reaches preadolescence, the parents do not change their approach to family government so as to allow the young person a role in family decision-making.
- As children acquire their new thinking capacity, parents do not take advantage of the fact that conflicts can now be thought through rather than always approached by trial and error.
- When families are operating destructively, parents often do not know how to change their style for the better. Lacking creative approaches to parenting, they get tougher with their young person, which often results in more conflict. This can go on for years, whereas some timely counsel could make a great deal of difference.

It is obvious to me that children must be taught to choose and to make wise choices. As mentioned previously, at about age 12—during preadolescence—young people are going to acquire new thinking abilities that allow them to think through their problems without first having to try out every solution. Along with these new capacities comes a need to have some power in family decisions—maybe a vote or a suggestion that is taken seriously.

Both Karen and Bob probably would have profited from being taught to deal with the realities of life at an early age. "People don't get everything they want." "Yes, sometimes we have to do things we don't feel like doing." "No, you can't go because we have other plans and you are part of those plans." "No, we don't have the money to do that." They also might have been helped by being part of a family meeting in which members are encouraged to voice their opinions and to give reasons for their ideas, perhaps very workable ones with slight modifications. Then when their thinking took on new dimensions, they could be ready for the increased challenge.

Chapter 10, on the "family council," is an expansion of these ideas and provides a method by which many families have been able to encourage their young people to take responsibility for their actions, and to think through their suggestions with the help of others. The family council assumes that the family is a primary learning center with the responsibility of challenging its members to grow. We the parents design this center, making it happen for better or worse.

NOTES

1. See Paul Mussen, John Janeway Conger, Jerome Kagan, *Child Development and Personality* (New York: Harper & Row, 1963), p. 313.

7. Stages of Adolescence

By the adolescent years, values or patterns of response are quite clearly etched. Burton White, a prominent child psychologist, says that even by age 3, personality is well along its way to full development.[1]

Living in Colorado, I have been able to observe some patterns in nature that have their parallels in people. It is an awesome experience to float on a raft down some of the rivers that wind their way through deep canyons, some more than a thousand feet deep. These canyons have not always been there. They have been gradually cut by the power in the water. Each century the rivers impress their patterns more deeply in the earth. Each year it becomes less and less likely that the river will alter its path. I have been awed by the power in these rivers. There is nothing they are unable to penetrate.

Behaviors, too, cut deep paths. Responses occur, are reinforced, and the same responses are likely to happen over and over again. These behaviors are soon predictable, for they form the basic response pattern of the personality. These behaviors we call values.

One extreme example, sort of the "Royal Gorge" type, dramatically illustrates my point. Bill learned early that feelings were to be kept to himself. "Boys don't cry" was a clear message to him. He learned either that he shouldn't have his own feelings or that he should feel what someone else expected him to feel.

Learning about feelings takes a long time. As the canyon is shaped by the river, so these personality traits, once established, are difficult to alter. By age 16, Bill had learned well. He was cool. He never let people know how he felt. He even fooled himself some of the time. An experienced observer, however, could spot Bill's feelings; they erupted in spite of his coverup. He was sarcastic. He put people down. He was rude, impatient, selfish—all expressions of his patterns.

In spite of his cool appearance, Bill could not hide his feelings. Like the river, his training had cut deep patterns. Certain situations elicited certain feelings within him; even when Bill wanted to change his feelings or values, he found it almost impossible. He reacted stubbornly to people, telling them what to do. I'm not sure how that started, but his mom saw it like this: "Bill always wanted his own way, and finally I just gave in. He was about 6 when I decided that. It wasn't worth the hassle. Why fight it? If I crossed him, he threw a tantrum, so I figured it was best to let him have his way."

One of his teachers saw it this way: "He was obnoxious in class, needing a lot of attention. He always had to show people that he was cool. I finally realized that no matter what I did, he was not going to cooperate. Finally, I couldn't fight it any longer, I just passed him."

The juvenile court judge put it this way: "Bill can't seem

to make it in his home town. Trouble seems to be his way of proving that he is somebody. He seems to have to constantly challenge the rules and do things his way."

Response patterns begin to etch their way into a child at the earliest age. They gradually gather momentum and erode their own canyon—for better or worse—as surely as the tiniest trickle of water becomes the mighty river. The job of a parent is one of a shaper, an engineer. The role shifts gradually over the years from giving complete hour-by-hour care, to standing by to consult when needed. The adolescent years require gentle but firm persistence, good humor, and courtesy.

Let's take a look at a three-way division of the adolescent years and see how each stage affects your role as a parent or as a child: ages 10 to 13, early adolescence; 14 to 15, transitional; 16 to 20, late adolescence. These ages could be grouped differently. I group them this way because of my own observation of young people. To me, certain themes are evident at these ages, though they certainly overlap and even continue into the next age. The ages here are meant to be guidelines for parents, not hard and fast laws of development.

AGES 10–13 (EARLY ADOLESCENCE, PHASE I)

I hesitate to use the word *chaos* here, but early adolescence can seem to be a topsy-turvy stage. Biological change starts the flow of intense feelings, a clue that life will never be the same. As mentioned earlier, these feelings challenge the young person and demand new coping devices. Impulsive, poorly thought out actions can often be the result of feelings that seem overwhelming. There is also evidence of awkwardness and rapid growth that may be comical in some respects; these can be very humiliating for the child, and equally exasperating for the parents.

"Jostling" is perhaps the best word to describe what goes on between ages 10 and 13. Young people jostle among themselves for position—to gain attention, acceptance, power, control. These early adolescents jostle each other as they become more and more sensitive, even *over* sensitive, to being accepted by their peers. At age 9 or 10, with the onset of sexual awareness, young people begin to think through their own approach to life in relation to what their parents have been telling them for the first 10 years of life. Sexual awareness makes life an even more individual experience than it was before. There is an uneasiness with boy-girl relationships, which are sometimes blown grotesquely out of proportion by rumors and false information about sexuality, which spreads widely via the "grapevine."

Since they have a strong desire to please, parents as well as peers, young adolescents can be easily hurt by remarks that they see as personal "put-downs." Because they are trying so hard to find their own place—wherever they are—they may resort to crude mechanisms, such as childish displays of stubborness or rebellion, as they struggle to fit a new experience, feeling, or person into thier old familiar system. This is a time when a low self-image can crystallize into behavior that is puzzling, at least, and sometimes even frightening.

Susan is 14. It is difficult to believe that a young woman receiving straight As in school could feel so badly about herself, but she does. For some reason, deep inside her is a hardcore belief that people like her because she does well in school. She feels somewhat like an outcast at school because she does so well, yet at home she feels the very same behavior brings her acceptance. One day Susan says:

> I feel sad all the time. I am afraid of people, afraid they won't like me. Sometimes I would just like to have fun, but I'm afraid I would be laughed at or that I would be clumsy, obnoxious, or

awkward. I just try to get through a day with no major disasters. I sometimes find myself wanting kids to make fun of me— the student—just so I will be noticed.

Her parents have noticed her spending time alone, not interested in doing things with the family or with friends. The awkwardness of her body changes, along with the pressures at school to compete for friends, have only intensified her self-condemnation. Her parents had hoped that adolescence would bring new friends and new opportunities, but this didn't seem to be happening; in fact, she seemed to be moving toward even greater isolation. Susan may need professional help before her patterns get too set. Emotions can be changed, but it takes consistent work.

Parents can help this change happen by working at being parents. This is a time when the courteous and friendly consideration of a parent will pay high dividends. Rick, a professional photographer, at age 30 looks back on his early adolescence and remembers how often his father took him along to help on a film production:

> I remember people relating to me as part of the production company—the sound man or anyone else on the crew. I felt about the same age as everybody else there. I had two worlds to choose from. I remember feeling like I was one of the grownups, but I didn't have to be responsible because I was still a kid. I could konk out and sleep behind the set—not sneakily, but knowing "I'm only a kid, it's okay to go to sleep." On the other hand, I felt that I was pretty essential, pretty special, doing my tasks with great concern. The responsibility that was given to me by my father—the trust, the faith—made me feel special. I always felt like I was part of something important, part of a bigger picture.

It is encouraging to realize that four out of five young people will make it through these preliminary years and pass into the next stage with a newly acquired sense of stability. Most young people do fall in a broad category between the extremes of perfect adjustment or social reject. For one out of five, however, this jostling ends up in real disruption. He or she will begin acting out feelings of isolation or withdrawal by searching for acceptance in a deviant subculture or retreating into some fantasy world. This young person will be in and out of mental hospitals or correctional institutions. Most of society does not know how to relate to this person, who becomes a social reject, unacceptable and passed by. The future for this young adult is dismal. Even though the statistics do not seem overwhelming, when that one out of five is yours, it is heartbreaking. A parent whose child seems endlessly trapped in mental hospitals or correctional agencies finds no solace in statistics and no comfort in knowing that they have four other children "doing all right."

Let's not play the statistics game blindly. A society with any troubled young people must dedicate itself to help those who have lost their way. For years now, I have observed communities that provide many services for children and for adults between 35 and 65 years old. The young people 12–24 and adults 65 and older are left out. When a 16-year-old becomes pregnant, we often take the easy attitude: "Maybe this will teach her," or "I guess she has to learn the hard way."

Keep in mind that crimes committed by a hurting young person hurt all of us and are a reflection on all of us; illegitimate pregnancies bring children into the world who might not have a family, or even one caring parent. If one is lost, we must band together to help find that one. Help comes in many forms: parenting classes; counseling services; halfway houses; crisis intervention teams; compassionate teachers, coaches, and youth leaders; and neighbors and friends who are willing to reach out and be supportive.

The Role of the Parent

The role of the parent changes at the onset of adolescence. It is a time when a great deal of information, support, and understanding is needed. Rick remembers his photographer father taking him along on many filming trips—on location to an Indian reservation, to the chemistry lab, to the locks on the river, to the recording session or the artist's studio. So much was taught in the sharing of the experience. No wonder we read that the most significant person in the life of an adolescent—for better or worse—is the parent.

Susan also remembers her parents during this time. Most of her friends left her alone, and she spent lots of time at home. Her mom saw Susan turning inward, and she decided not to let this happen. She began taking Susan along, doing things together, insisting that Susan get out. Mom would not take no for an answer, nor would she give in to Susan's apparent lack of interest or her occasional verbal abuse. Mom had decided, correctly, that Susan was hurting inside and that she needed someone to care for her regardless of her behavior. This was to become a turning point in Susan's life.

"Gifts are significant, too," Rick observes. "When I was 13, my father bought me a Pentax camera. I thought, 'He must trust me a lot!' He also let me use his darkroom and I felt it was mine as much as it was his. He'd tell me how to do everything, and then let me do it myself. I guess the best part, though, was when I made a mistake or ruined something, he never made me feel stupid." Though gifts may sometimes be an attempt to buy love, they can provide an opportunity to extend trust and to bond two people together in a mutual adventure.

While parents still take a lot of control during early adolescence, and often need to be directive, they must also allow the child some freedom to learn and to fail so that the patterns developing can be positive ones. Correct information, along with a supportive relationship of love and encouragement, will pay rich dividends as the adolescent continues to grow through both failing and succeeding.

In summary, there are two major shifts in the parent role during early adolescence:

- The parent encourages participation in family decision making, and is willing to give lots of support and direction that is right for all family members.
- The parent decides to spend time participating in the individual interests of the young person. Doing things together provides a model for the young person as well as support and encouragement to try new or difficult things.

AGES 14–15 (TRANSITION)

By this middle stage, the young person has been a part of the youth culture long enough to have settled into a social pattern, a place that begins to feel OK. It begins to have recognizable rules, shape, and form. Just as jostling characterized the first stage of adolescence, *settling in* marks this second stage—settling into a familar pattern in the peer culture.

Healthy young people at this age are beginning to realize their strengths and weaknesses, their personal uniqueness. They are beginning to develop a style in relating to others that builds up their strengths and seeks to do something about the weaknesses. There is a willingness to stretch and to learn, because they sense that there will be a "pulling up roots" time not too far in the future and, in some ways, a breaking away from the familiar primary family unit.

Since adolescent patterns of relationship are developing at this stage, it is a prime time to learn some of the important ingredients of friendship. Though the roots of intimacy were planted much earlier in the private soil of the family, now is the time for experiment with intimacy—from secrets to sex to prayer—between peers, and perhaps with an adult friend.

New reasoning abilities have also made it possible and exciting to plan thoroughly, and to consider the consequences of these plans. There is a time for planning things together and for letting each person be responsible to carry out his or her part of the plan. The parent role shifts from a more directive authority to a partner and friend.

Young people who have found development difficult during the 10 to 13 years, may, by age 14, begin to adapt to their surroundings in a negative way. Some feel trapped by parents or school, which is dull and boring compared to life "out there." Their need for excitement and curiosity leads to the risky edge of adventure, especially for those who are fed up with their families and run away. Their direction may take them into drug abuse, easy money games, indiscriminate sex practices, or even prostitution.

A tenth-grade girl in Indiana wrote to me:

> When I was 14, my home life was terrible. My younger sisters and brothers were always ganging up against me. I couldn't tell my problems to my mother because she'd go and tell the neighbors. I couldn't take it any longer, so I ran away.
>
> They got me back, and my punishment was that I couldn't date till I turned 17. It's still no picnic at home, but I have a boyfriend I can talk to. He listens and helps me. I've only got two more years at home, and I'm doing pretty well.[2]

Two Problem Types

Among the 14- and 15-year-olds I see at the Dale House, I note two types of troubled young people. One, young people who feel rejected, and see themselves as "throwaways." In their 14 or 15 years of living, they have not learned the basic skills of being independent in our society; there is a sense of hopelessness about them. Some are so far behind in developing these skills that they try all kinds of coping mechanisms. Bluffing is a common one: "I could make it at school if I wanted to," they'll say. Or, "I'll just find a job. It won't be any problem." They settle in to a pattern of bluffing, rather than acquiring the basic skills needed to make it for the rest of life.

It isn't easy to get through to the young bluffer. These kids have been hurt deeply, and for a long period of time. There is a kind of calloused crustiness that forms around their spirit of living. Yet the crust must be cracked; and many of these young people have to hit bottom before they begin to rebound and start to work at developing the skills they'll need in adulthood.

The second type of troubled young person is the one who has gotten through ages 10 to 13 and arrives at age 14 with an aggressive personality oriented to self-satisfaction. These young people are often into their own thing, and will agree to anything as long as their needs are met. Like the first type, they almost need to hit bottom before they begin to respond to the demands of life in a productive way. Part of the reason for this kind of trouble is that parents may not have allowed these young people to participate in the reality of life. Parents often have not taken the time to give them a taste of what life is really like and have not allowed them to participate actively in it. These young people often have not had much to say in the family.

Like the bluffers, these adolescents are hard to crack. Their personal needs for love and affection are so great that they are not able to give to others; and until some of these needs are met, they will continue in their self-seeking lifestyle. Though these people are very vulnerable to drugs, sexual exploitation, and crime, it will probably be a loving, uncondemning adult who will finally "break through."

The more aggressive individuals at this stage have gone out and attacked life in the peer culture and have found not only that they can survive, but that they can get a lot of excitement out of doing it. The peer culture, however, is not total reality; and in the larger world these blustery, egocentric, aggressive facades may pop open with the dawning realization that apartment living costs money, jobs are hard to come by, and developing competent marketable skills in certain areas is not the same as getting through school.

In summary, this transition stage—ages 14 and 15—is a marvelous time to try and to fail, because of the significant learning that goes with this process. While 10–13 is, in some ways, a time for laying a foundation for new personal values, 14 and 15 is a time to start living out these values in the supportive framework of the family. The next stage, a time for pulling up roots, may work a little more smoothly if the demands of the big world have been rehearsed under the watchful guidance of the family, always with the realization that without a chance to try and fail, there is no real exercise of strength.

The Role of the Parent

The role of the parent during this second stage is one of sharing life and responsibility. Parents can help their children live out their newly discovered strengths and weaknesses. They can encourage and evaluate. They need to be on hand to help them measure how they are doing. They may need to say, "I know you're not making it like you want to in your job. Let's try something else. How about quitting for awhile and thinking about it?" At this stage, parents become consultants, not so directive, but helping to ask the questions and assisting in finding the answers.

A tenth-grade girl wrote to me from Kentucky, "My parents were on my back all the time. They just wouldn't let me grow up. I became paranoid. I thought they hated me. One night I broke down and told them how I felt. They were stubborn, but they heard me through. I think the entire neighborhood heard me too. For a while, my parents continued to yell or ignore me, but gradually they've started to listen, and it showed me they care. This last year I've begun to fill the communication gap with my folks."[3]

Recently I heard a mother say, "Nan's starting to fight back, and we're finally beginning to learn what's going on inside of her. Before, there was always a point where I could see the wall go up in her eyes, and she'd walk out and go to her room. One day I just screamed at her, 'Nan! What are you thinking? Please tell me.' " That was the turning point in that family. The exploration has begun, and new understanding is opening up.

This is a prime time for parents to support, to supplement, to model real-life involvement for their children in the very best way they know. This is not necessarily easy, but it can be a stretching, stimulating, growth-producing time for the adults as well as for the teenagers.

For the parents of a young person who is troubled, this is the time for active intervention. This will be difficult, but it is imperative. Destructive styles of relating have crystallized somewhat, and it will not be easy to break through this crustiness. Don't try to kid yourself that everything will be all right tomorrow.

One family chased their 15-year-old daughter from crash pad to crash pad for six months. They were determined not to let her be totally destroyed. While tracking her down, they were in and out of psychiatrists' offices, the police station, juvenile hall, and any other mental-health facility they thought might help. For them it paid off; for many it does not, but it is the right thing to try.

Many parents give up on this age group. Early adolescence has been trying for them. Their young people have been acting impulsively and have been verbally abusive for too long. Their new reasoning abilities have only enabled them to be more devious and sophisticated in their schemes to get what they want. It's just too much, and a mutual agreement to leave each other alone develops.

I can understand this, and I am sympathetic with both sides, as both usually have done their part to bring it on. However, it is a costly compromise, where both parties lose. These severe cases usually demand outside intervention, which is becoming more available, and it must be sought.

In summary, the parent's role continues to shift during this transition period in the following ways:

- The parent becomes more of a consultant, co-worker, or partner in family discussions and planning. When events are scheduled that take some planning, each person is challenged to be responsible for his or her part of the plan.
- Problems will not be outgrown, but need to be faced head-on with every effort made to overcome them in a constructive manner.

AGES 16–20 (LATE ADOLESCENCE, PHASE II)

The key word for these years is *independence,* and this stage is often referred to as *pulling up roots.* This is the age when a young person makes an extra effort to become independent and self-supportive. Skills, such as money handling, personal grooming, housekeeping, and cooking, which have been practiced under supervision, now start to run on their own steam.

While all of the time since childhood has been designed to help the person become independent, these are the years when the balance moves further toward the side of independence. More time is spent outside of the home; friends who are new to the parents are brought home to be introduced; plans are laid to go to work or college; and summers are spent away from home, working or at camp.

Three important developments of this stage of adolescence are (1) an openness and a desire to learn more about living; (2) an attempt to build serious relationships, which have the potential of becoming life-long friendships, with both the same and the opposite sex; (3) an effort to look into the type of training needed for vocation. The pulling-up-roots stage is a time when a person is seeking personal goals. It is often a highly competitive stage, a time when discipline pays off in adulthood.

The young person seeks out opportunities to satisfy a curiosity about life. New interest areas may be explored briefly by means of a trip; a summer job; some volunteer work at a hospital, or working with the elderly, the deprived, or disadvantaged young people. Often driven by a type of idealism, the young person can become much more realistic about life and its problems after some of these experiences. Parents get involved with these plans, providing encouragement and new ideas. It can be a growing time of working and planning together, which actually helps develop a new closeness.

Interests in common and similar lifestyles bring young people together in friendships that could continue. Friendships with the opposite sex also begin to suggest the possibility of permanence. Parents who have been close to their young people continue to be important as this happens. Friends and potential marriage partners become part of the family, and the family plays a vital role in helping its members develop friendships or choose partners with whom they can share the rest of their lives.

For our society, late adolescence is a time to decide on future plans for education, training, or work. Families help in these decisions. This is a time to ask questions and to look at all possibilities. Parents can provide great support, along with practical wisdom, to a young person facing these choices.

Pulling up roots is like any other stage of growth; it is not automatically constructive for all concerned. It must be worked on carefully and planned for if it is to be successful. A lot of the fun, in fact, is in the planning.

The young person who enters this stage troubled is often overwhelmed with frustrations, lack of direction, and either a desire to get help if possible or a callousness to the need for help. Unlike the 14- or 15-year-old, many 17- and 18-year-olds will realize they are in trouble and that help is necessary. During this stage, the curiosity and excitement of two or three years spent in the drug scene may be revealed as a routine of merely drifting with unachieved goals. The old ideal of endless satisfaction may turn into a nightmare of just getting from one day to the next.

However, for the older adolescent two or three years out of school or near failure in school, help may be complicated. In addition, any number of legal hassles, lost jobs, or alienation from family and friends may have left a tough tangle of emotional problems.

Ken is 18, with a resistance to learning and a superior attitude toward most adults. He has used the line, "I can do it if I only apply myself," so long that he now believes it. He is deluded. His parents believed it for awhile, but now they are sick of it and they can't get through to Ken. Even Fs in school are explained away: "I missed too many classes." Test scores are denied: "I did better, they just scored it wrong." Ken is convinced he is a genius waiting to be found.

His skin is so thick that penetration may be impossible. Confrontation, even with obvious, blatant facts, brings denial and lies. Ken has lost himself in a tangle of emotional confusion. He has two choices: go on living in a dream world or face the failure and begin a long road to recovery. For Ken, the dream seems easier now.

The Role of the Parent

Except in the case of emotional trouble, parents of 16- to 20-year-olds take on the role of partner or consultant. At this stage, they stand by to give help and support when asked. They try to make it clear, "I'm here to help if you need me." One common fault in our society comes from trying to insulate these young people from every kind of disappointment or difficulty. This age group needs the freedom to fail.

Teacher and author Ann Kiemel wrote in the March 1976 *Campus Life* magazine:

> My parents allowed me to be vulnerable to life's disappointments. They did not protect me from pain. For years they had built a solid foundation of a loving God in me, and then they dared me to open wide my enthusiasm to be and to do and to give. They cared for my bruises with dignity. I have always healed, in time. . . . I have known defeat: a speech tournament, a queen's court, a job rejection, a romance. . . . I am grateful for defeat. It is life and life is where people live.[4]

Wise parents learn to progress from the role of strong leader, to sharing responsibility, to being a friend and consultant in the sweet-and-sour adventure of life. In our society, it still seems that the two greatest needs a young person feels are for a parent and for a friend.

Faced with helping a troubled young person in late adolescence, parents feel everything from hopelessness, to excitement and joy, to panic and despair. Negative patterns being expressed by the young adult suggest a frightening possibility of permanence. Apathy, hostility, or self-destructive behavior seem to have settled in at times. At other times, a glimpse of light, such as going back to school, holding a job for six months, or an act of kindness toward the parents, explodes into excitement, which is quickly harnessed to avoid a "too happy" appearance. This continual "egg walking" leaves parents drained and wondering if this is how life was intended. There are, however, few good alternatives at this time, and giving up is not one of them.

The hopeful parent acknowledges a need for help, lives honestly, and refuses to pamper, excuse, or bail the young person out of trouble. Support, yes! Love, yes! But a bottomless well of financial support or "pull" with city officials, NO!

NOTES

1. Burton White, *The First Three Years of Life* (Englewood Cliffs, N.J.: Prentice-Hall, 1975).
2. From "Feedback Column" in *Co-Ed*, March 1977, in response to Oraker, "Can a Runaway Go Home?" *Co-Ed*, December 1976, p. 46.
3. Ibid.
4. Ann Kiemel, "A Stab I Can Never Forget," an excerpt from *I Love the Word Impossible, Campus Life*, March 1976, p. 33.

8. Guidelines for Growth and Understanding

Does it feel like too much? Please don't stop here. Look at it this way: You are still being shaped, and hopefully improved in the process! Life at its best is a never-ending involvement, and boredom's greatest enemy is continous growth. Futility and frustration may retreat as you open one door after another—for your child and for yourself.

The young person can approach adolescence in one of two general ways: chaotically, expecting and dealing with one crisis after another; or eagerly, understanding it as a normal, natural growth experience.

PUTTING THE PUZZLE TOGETHER

Research psychologist R. R. Carkhuff,[1] helps us identify some steps to try in working through difficulties to insure personal growth. Do you wonder what to do when, for instance, John is coming home drunk? Barbara is intentionally throwing up to stay slim? Greg is withdrawing to his room, talking less, seeming to be shy or perhaps grim? Molly is staying out long past the agreed on time for being in, defiant, abusive to her parents, and acting out her defiance sexually? Dad is rigid with the kids, hostile, demanding and impossible to talk to? Mom is threatening to leave?

Carkhuff suggests three steps to take in helping relationships.[2] I find them extremely useful: (1) *exploration*, (2) *understanding*, and (3) *action*. Try them out and see how they will serve you as guidelines for "working at family."

These stages in communication can best be illustrated by a jigsaw puzzle. On occasion, when our family would get together for some special event, someone would go to the closet and bring out a jigsaw puzzle. Though we came to know the puzzles quite well, they never seemed to lose their excitement or intrigue. The most difficult puzzles were the round ones with the very small pieces, especially if they were new and we had no picture to show us what the final puzzle should look like. Someone would dump the puzzle into the center of the room, and we would all form a circle around the pile of pieces. Then began the task of exploring the pieces, looking for clues that would help us put the puzzle together. The first stage, *exploring*, is one of sifting through the pieces to find those with edges, corners, or some color or unique marking that match each other.

During this exploration stage, getting to know someone or trying to help someone solve a problem is a similar process of sifting. No specific direction is established. Questions are asked. Emotions are expressed, sorted out, and considered. Opinions are weighed to see whether or not they point us in a certain direction. As we sift through the pieces, we eventually find those that fit together; as more and more pieces fit, we begin to understand what some part of the puzzle represents.

Understanding is the second stage of putting together the puzzle. Sections of the puzzle fit together and aha! we see a waterwheel in the righthand corner or some animals playing. Now we begin to understand the picture more, and our direction is becoming clearer. Next we look for pieces that will tie these sections together and eventually make the puzzle complete.

Family situations are much like this. As we explore the various parts of a family dilemma, we gain a greater understanding on which to base a decision. Thus, we can plan for appropriate *action* on the basis of our understanding. Let's look, for instance, at the problem of choosing a family vacation. Tommy, who is 6, would like to have something to say about where the family spends its vacation. Sally, who is 16, would like to help her parents understand that she might benefit from *not* going on the family vacation this summer. Mom would like people to know that she needs help in planning their clothes for the vacation. It is also helpful to know what everybody is expecting out of this two weeks of the year. In short, this process of sifting and understanding before acting makes a great deal of sense. It is a very simple, step-by-step technique for making almost any family decision. It shows respect for each member of the family and understanding of the needs of each member. It also demonstrates a desire that each member be allowed to grow and develop according to his or her various age-level needs.

Stage I—Exploration

It takes time to find people; they must be explored and gradually discovered. The process is like a miner sifting and picking, carefully examining each piece of rock for its hidden treasure; or a scientist doggedly testing and retesting each possible plan; or a geologist charting each bend of the river, each rock formation, looking for clues to origin and history. Finding people also is a never-ending adventure. Each feeling, attitude, or talent suggests rich reservoirs to be tapped, reservoirs full of fear, joy, anger, excitement, despair, grief, and happiness.

Family members need to explore each other. Parents can aid in this adventure of discovery by being available when a child needs to talk, needs holding, or needs to be confronted. During this stage of helping, the helper is a friend who listens, supports, asks thoughtful questions, and then helps sift through all the pieces that emerge.

You may have a Lisa in your home—frustrated, feeling penned in by parents and pressured by friends. The Lisa I know is 17. To her, life seemed like a pressure cooker, building steam daily. She was tense; her "fuse" was short. She snapped at everybody and seemed impossible to live with. Her mom, almost at her wits' end, sat down one night and asked if Lisa would let her listen to anything she wanted to say. Tears filled Lisa's eyes. "Nobody understands," she began. "Dad just lays on the rules. My friends are wanting more and more of my time. And I feel like I'm going to burst! Nobody understands."

This was at 9:00 in the evening. At 3:00 the next morning, Mom and Lisa turned in—exhausted, uncertain, knowing little more than the fact that Lisa had talked and Mom had listened. Though there were no solutions or even suggestions of solutions, they both felt a little better. In fact, this was only the beginning of a long sifting and exploring friendship. But there was new hope. Both decided to be patient and to get to know each other. They knew it would take time, but they were committed to a new relationship.

Gradually this journey took them into Lisa's feelings of

rejection, of not measuring up to either parents or peers. It also took them into Mom's fear of losing Lisa, her desire to protect her, and her tendency to want to live out her own dreams through this 17-year-old. The sifting had started, and there were many clues that new intimacy lay just around the corner. A feeling that things would work out—only a feeling—suggested that the next stage of a truly helpful relationship was about to begin. The excitement of "birth" was accompanied by pain and the uneasy awareness that each one of them now knew a great deal about the other and could, if they chose to misuse their new information, cause a lot of trouble for the other. Exploration, true exploration, can be painful, tedious, exhausting. Many find it too difficult. But those who are willing to stretch their old energies will be rewarded.

Stage II—Understanding

As the personality pieces come to the surface, some fit together and make sense. Others drift alone, finding no place to settle in. The ones that do fit provide the beginnings of new insight into understanding the person or the problem. We begin to see why Tom's father is so critical, why Barbara is so worried about her grades, why Eddie has no friends, or why Sally is afraid of not being liked.

As Lisa and Mom continued to dredge up the pieces, they began to see that the family rules made Lisa feel like a child. She got a new sense of her parents' sincerity, but, at the same time, she saw that she needed to help decide what her part in the family was. Mother realized that it was important to trust Lisa; it was necessary that she let Lisa be responsible. They also began to discover together that Mom was strict because the more Lisa became independent, the more Mom felt she was losing her "little girl." This made her feel grief, futility, rejection. Whenever she began feeling those feelings, she responded by treating Lisa as "just a child" who needed her mother's guidance.

Lisa and Mom both gained new understanding and new appreciation of each other. Lisa's outbursts no longer threatened Mom, rather, they were recognized as a reminder that Lisa needed a friend—right now. And Mom's intrusive efforts to structure Lisa's time were greeted with, "Okay, Mom, let's talk." Their new understanding of each other felt good, like a secret they shared. They saw how much each needed what the other knew, and they were willing to accept the challenge of trying to dig out those thoughts and feelings and put them into words.

Until a degree of more complete understanding is achieved, moving into the action stage is bound to be frustrating, if not disastrous. Action often results in poor plans that fail. Why? Because the problem has never been defined accurately. When Plan A fails, some parents are quick to implement Plan B, which can be worse yet. On the other hand, plans that grow out of responses to understanding have a better chance of being successful as well as helpful.

Stage III—Action

"I've spent six months understanding my problem; won't somebody help me figure out what to do about it?"

There are many reasons for such a statement, I suppose; in any case, it is a plea to get going. Some teenagers may be anxiously avoiding real understanding. Some are pleading with the counselor or parent to "please take responsibility for my problem." Others are ready for action. The best action plans, as previously stated, are formed out of understanding. The patterns of behavior are more clear, and problems can be traced to some of their underlying causes or at least to situations that seem to cause them.

Lisa and her mom had become aware of each other's feelings and of the situations most likely to stimulate these feelings. They agreed to help each other during these times by noticing each other's needs and insisting that they get together during these times. They also planned to take some action: to do something together each week, such as lunch or a walk in the park, that would provide an opportunity to talk. This would keep conflict from building up and would very likely result in a better relationship. Since they both felt that this would help to solve the problem, they were gladly committed to make the plan work.

Carkhuff tells us that these stages go on, endlessly cycling as a relationship grows and develops, each stage leading to the next, which eventually leads back to the first. Exploration leads to understanding, which leads to action, which creates a need for more exploration.

With this cycle, relationships seldom grow stale or become boring. Each day brings new challenges and discoveries as another thread in the tapestry of life is woven. Lots of surprises, lots of unexplained moments whose meaning may be hidden in a sense of trust, lots of emotion. Even the sharp edge of grief splits the air occasionally, driving to the very soul of a relationship. Tears mysteriously fuse individuals together in deep intimacy. Family relationships take on continuously new dimensions as each person is seen as a lifelong quest.

NOTES

1. R. R., Carkhuff, *The Art of Helping* III (Amherst, Mass.: Human Resources Development Press, 1977.

2. Carkhuff, p. i.

9. Family as Community

The description of community in the New Testament has marvelous implications for families. It appears significantly different from the behaviorist approach to an engineered family, and from the client-centered, self-centered approach. In fact, though Carl Rogers's *On Personal Power*[1] sounds free and personally fulfilling, in my opinion, this view is alienating when compared with a biblical view of community. Let's take a look at some important biblical ingredients of an effective family, as well as some of the false substitutes that many accept in the place of a healing community.

In a New Testament community, there is a deep involvement in each others' lives:

> All the believers continued together in close fellowship and shared their belongings with one another. They would sell their property and possessions, and distribute the money among all, according to what each one needed. Day after day they met as a group in

the Temple, and they had their meals together in their homes, eating with glad and humble hearts, praising God, and enjoying the good will of all the people. (Acts 2:44–45, Good News)

One aspect of this involvement is the commitment of love as seen in Romans 12:10, (Phillips-New Testament in Modern English) which involves a challenge to live together in *harmony:* "Let us have real warm affection for one another as between brothers, and a willingness to let the other man have the credit." Love in the New Testament community is a decision that is not based solely on feelings. Love is a decision to be committed to a person. It involves work and sacrifice. Feeling "warm fuzzies" for a person has little to do with the New Testament definition of agape love; likewise, living in harmony does not mean that there is no discord. Many see avoiding the hassle as harmony, but it is only an inadequate substitute. Discord, in fact, may in the long run produce genuine harmony and consistent growth, whereas avoiding hassles can lead to pooled hostility that will destroy community. Love involves commitment to people and involvement in their lives; harmony only evolves out of conflict that is resolved.

I remember a young man who periodically appeared on the porch of the Dale House "strung out on drugs" or undernourished, dirty, and exhausted from weeks of living in crash pads. Dave was on his own by mutual agreement: he was too much of a continual frustration for his mom, and home was too restrictive for him, so he left. Dave was always into some new fad that promised instant healing but that never seemed to come. When he was in real trouble, he would call home collect and ask Mom to send money or a plane ticket, which she did. Even though her generosity only increased his trouble, she did it anyway. I don't blame her; I probably would have done the same. But it was wrong.

One night Dave came in to the Dale House with a handful

of pills. He had been told that if he did this once more, he would be asked to leave. When we told him to get rid of the pills, he quickly swallowed them, daring the staff to throw him out. It was a cold winter night in Colorado Springs, and Dave figured no one would be that cruel. He was wrong. Dave, a sleeping bag, and his packed suitcase were placed on the porch surrounded by snow. A staff person stayed with him. Dave screamed and pounded on the door in the middle of the night until we had to call the police. We had no choice but to hang tough with Dave in the situation. It was a strengthening decision for all of us.

My own decision in love is to commit myself to those— my family *and* my community—who, like me, are growing. I want what is best for me and for them, and I will work hard with them to make it happen. I know that living together produces a great deal of conflict, and I am committed to working through differences. I am convinced that a love that works through conflict is the first and most important ingredient of a growth-producing family.

I am convinced that love based solely on my feelings, and harmony based on merely avoiding discord, are inadequate substitutes for New Testament love and harmony in our society. Even though my own needs and desires are important, I must work at not "buying into" a cheap philosophy of selfishness—taking the easy way out and avoiding conflict at any cost. There is a great deal of this attitude today in marriages and in families with teenagers. For some reason, "avoiding the hassle" is a common phrase. This philosophy does not build a healthier community, nor is it biblical. Rather we must learn to "speak the truth in love" (Ephesians 4:15, RSV), some powerful advice for families that means to speak truthfully in a manner that communicates clearly to others and takes into account their emotional needs.

A second ingredient of community is the willingness to "bear one another's burdens." This teaching in the Bible focuses on being aware of the needs of others. I am told to care for others and to help them bear their burdens (Galatians 6:2; 1 Corinthians 12:25)—ways of reaching out that are very powerful.

The injunction "to care" is not limited to crisis cases, when troubles demand attention. Our society tends to mobilize quickly in emergencies; we seem to have "crisis lines" for just about every possible crisis—drugs, divorce, suicide, obesity, alcoholism. In the day-to-day routine however, the attitude tends to be, "I have enough problems of my own. Don't bother me, I'm too busy." In a family that is truly a community, burdens are shared; in fact, there is a desire to care for one another. Members of these communities actually look for ways to be helpful, even to the point of self-sacrifice. It is a strange dynamic, but when this kind of caring occurs, all people are blessed.

Though humanistic psychology encourages us to be sensitive to each other and to facilitate and care for each other, a concept that is certainly biblical in its thrust, the motivation is different. For the Christian, love is a power that enables us to act. It is the chief motivator in relationships. This love helps us obey. In biblical community, we are told to care and to bear one another's burdens, thus fulfilling God's law. It is a matter of obedience. My responsibility as a burden bearer apparently is woven right into God's most basic plan for me. As I worship him, he gives me the power of love to reach out to others. And when I do obey and care for another, something divine is taking place for both of us.

A third ingredient in a biblical community is forgiveness and forbearance (Ephesians 4:2, 32). The modern attitude of "live and let live," along with an ever-growing emphasis on "getting back at" a person is an inadequate substitute. Forgetting or ignoring people or situations does not accomplish what forgiveness accomplishes in a relationship. When I fail miserably, or when I hurt someone, I need to be forgiven. I do not need to be ignored, or tolerated, or gotten even with. Somehow, I can grow and learn when I am forgiven. I feel the exhilaration of a fresh new space where I can accept my responsibility to others and the challenge to look at myself carefully—to face my failure and make some well-thought-out decisions about my future actions. Forgiveness is essential in families; it frees each person to grow.

Of course, a biblical concept of forgiveness involves a repentant heart. Sometimes we extend forgiveness even when a person has not requested it, for we can detect a sense of sorrow. Often, however, we continue to "beat people over the head" when they ask forgiveness just to remind them of what they have done to us. To forgive is a loving act that needs to happen in families. It helps produce loving people who have experienced grace from each other. Anything short of forgiveness, such as tolerance and forgetting, are inadequate substitutes. There is nothing that can replace the healing of repentance and forgiveness.

Forbearance can be translated as "hanging in there." It is an attitude of being a friend even in unattractive situations. There is a natural tendency in our society to be attracted to "attractive" people or to people who produce. Others who are not so attractive are pushed aside as they serve no meaningful purpose. This attitude reveals some deep needs in those of us trapped by it. The Bible encourages us to hang in there with each other, even when we are depressed, obnoxious, impulsive, or boring to be with. Society's encouragement to surround yourself only with people you like is again a costly substitute, draining off the true joy of helping someone who is having a hard time and who is not "fun" to be with.

A fourth ingredient of biblical community or family is submission to one another; that is, yielding and adapting to others in the family (Ephesians 5:21). This mode may appear to be passive, weak, and a compromise of personal dignity, because we live in a society that says take control, be assertive and confront. Before we get too simplistic or absolute, however, let's admit that there are two sides of this coin. First, to submit to something you know to be wrong would be highly destructive and, therefore, a type of conduct to be avoided. On the other hand, a willingness to put yourself in a position of serving, or facilitating the growth of another, would not be destructive and is certainly an important and constructive dynamic of healthy family. Thus, submission to the best interest of the group, rather than holding on to one's own advancement, is entirely different and is a core element in community.

Most rigid hierarchies, which place one person in a position of absolute authority over others, are contrary to the biblical teaching on community. Autocratic power, which is one rather popular interpretation for marriages, potentially facilitates oppression, bitterness, and even anger, which is contrary to the biblical teaching on what the effects of a community experience should be. The autocrat makes decisions on the basis of what he or she thinks is best for the other person. The biblical model seems to be one of servant leadership, even for those in power. The servant-leader involves the other person in the decision, and they carry it out together.

The passage concerning submission to the welfare of others (Philippians 2) certainly is not a model for being lorded over and forced to "knuckle under":

Your life in Christ makes you strong, and his love comforts you. You have fellowship with the Spirit, and you have kindness and compassion for one another. I urge you, then, to make me completely happy by having the same thoughts, sharing the same love, and being one in soul and mind. Don't do anything from selfish ambition or from a cheap desire to boast, but be humble toward one another, always considering others better than yourselves. And look out for one another's interest, not just for your own. The attitude you should have is the one that Christ Jesus had. (Philippians 2:1–5, Good News)

The stronger submits willingly for the purpose of serving the weaker. It is the serving, rather than a deliberate power play, that causes true Lordship. Submission or servant-leadership is a powerful dynamic in a healthy family, whereas passiveness and autocratic or authoritarian leadership are merely substitutes that look like community, but fall far short of what could happen.

A fifth ingredient of a family community is teaching and counseling, even reproving. "Teach and instruct one another with all wisdom" (Colossians 3:16, Good News). Families are to be laboratories for learning for each family member. In families, the teaching can be concrete and specific, much like the discipleship model in the Bible. It is not like the latest seminar or convention where the teachers are generalists, providing "a little something" for everyone. In both the Old Testament model of the great tradition passed on through families and the New Testament model of the body of Christians living in community, we see a pattern of commitment to pass on the rich purposes of life from one generation to another, and from one person to another. Families focus on the specifics of their members—"I learn as I relate specifically to real people in real situations, where I am related to as a person."

Admonition or friendly rebuke is also part of healthy family dynamics. The assumption that "what I do is my own business" may be rampant in our society; however, it does not ultimately lead to constructive growth, but rather to isolation and loneliness. Even a good humanist would gasp quietly at thinking of a society totally free of admonition. "Maybe I am not totally responsible for you, but I sure am going to say something if you continue to violate me." The Bible seems to be saying that admonition is a responsibility of a family member. In fact, it is often a measure of how much we love and how much we are willing to risk in the best interest of the other person.

The assumption that "what I do is my own business" is not a biblical concept, though many people operate this way. If I am committed to you, I will be involved with you; at least, I will be willing to struggle with you. Then we can decide whose business it is. In a caring community, what you do is my business because it affects me directly.

A sixth ingredient of Christian family is the encouragement and building up of one another. "So encourage one another, and help one another" (I Thessalonians 5:11, Good News). Virginia Satir in her book *Peoplemaking*[2] shows that self-image is closely related to communication in the family. Positive, affirming attitudes, along with realistic critical feedback, build people up and make them feel important.

FAMILY COMMUNICATION IS IMPORTANT

The patterns of communication in many families are full of put-downs, excessive teasing, sarcasm, and cynicism. Not only do these patterns hurt as they occur, but over a long period of time they become fact: "If I'm no good like you say, I might as well be no good."

To encourage one another means to give support and to aid or help. Along with all the rest I have said, I know that this makes parenting seem awesome. It is little wonder that some family experts see parents as commissioned to the important and delicate task of managing a factory for making people. The task is further complicated by our complex society. It is not an easy thing to guide your teenagers and at the same time let them learn by experience.

For example, Barbara was persuaded in early adolescence to think that her parents knew little about what was good for her. She was going to do what she wanted to do, which usually meant doing just the opposite of what her parents suggested. She went from high school pot parties to staying out all night. Finally, she ran away from home.

Barbara's parents were told by some friends to let her go. "She'll find out how tough life can really be. After all, most kids come home eventually," they were told. Unfortunately, we know too much about what could happen to Barbara to just "let her learn from experience." The risk is too great, even though most runaways do come home and many troubled young people do hit the bottom before they begin getting better.

Barbara's parents decided to do everything they could to get her back. They checked in with the police, checked out one crash pad after another. When they found her, they did everything they could to turn her life around. She was belligerent and defiant but finally consented to try. That consent was the first step. Eventually, Barbara did make it—thanks to parents who cared, parents who found the right people and places for help. Many young people, however, are not as fortunate as Barbara.

Another example is Robert, who dropped out of college in his sophomore year to see the country and get away from the system. Three years later, he is embarrassed to go back into classes with younger people. He is untrained and cannot find a job, yet he must work to support himself and can't go to school even if he wants to. It seems to him that he has wasted three years of his life, and he is a little depressed as he looks at the future. No one was able to get to Robert. His judgment was poor, and he is suffering the consequences of his actions. Now he will have to work hard to catch up, but his parents are still willing to help him. He can do it. Many universities and colleges are designing programs for the premature dropout, and Robert will probably get back on the track.

Cindy's parents had told her to get out, and she did. The feeling was mutual, and she was not going back for anyone. After staying at a half-way house for a time when she was 16, with some support from the county she moved out into independent living. She was not able to manage. Cindy had very few skills for the basic tasks of life. Budgeting, cooking, holding down a job, attending school, all were overwhelming to her. Her money went fast, the rent was due, and she looked hard for a way out.

One of Cindy's friends was "working the boulevard" and seemed to be making good money. She saw the chance to pay the rent and have some nice things, so she met her "man" and began to work. Had she had any idea of what awaited her, she would have done anything else. Now just one year later, Cindy is bitter, hard, calloused, angry, and considerably older physically than her 17 years.

Though many young people can recover and gain the skills needed for adulthood, Cindy's story is tragic. In one short year, she has worn out her emotional systems—they were never designed for such abuse—and she may spend the rest of her life trying to prove to herself that she is worthwhile. Of course, Cindy is worthwhile; of course, Jesus loves Cindy and died for her. There is no one too lost for salvation and redemption, but Cindy, as much as anyone, needs a friend.

When do I let my child learn by experience and when do I step in and say a firm "NO"? As we have seen, some young people are not able to make good judgments, and the risk of experiment is great. Other young people can handle responsibility and need the freedom to manage their lives and to learn from their mistakes. For these, the risk is low, and they can profit from their experiences. Parents must provide each child with the atmosphere most likely to encourage growth.

Growth, as we have seen, takes place in relationships that I refer to as community. This community is a God-intended part of life; even in creation we are told we cannot live alone (Genesis 2:13), and the family, or community, takes on God-ordained significance. This chapter was written to point out some ingredients that seem to be important in Scripture and in our positive development. Although society may encourage us to live a certain way, it often is not God's best for us.

GROWTH IS A TWO-WAY EXPERIENCE

The job of parenting a young adult is both important and satisfying. Much of the satisfaction comes from the excitement and adventure of a truly functioning biblical community in action. During this time of life, for both the parent and the young person, growth is a two-way experience. Bonds of friendship are developing to replace the old parent-child bonds. For some, these bonds never do develop, leaving both somewhat frustrated and incomplete.

Burton White has found that "at least for the first three years of a child's life, most families have adequate resources to rear him well."[3] However, families usually find that as their children grow older, the task of parenting is not so natural or automatic. The family with adolescents often urgently needs additional resources to cope with situations. This is a challenging time in the life of a family, for both parents and young people.

The challenge is to work hard to live out the healthy principles of biblical community—being committed to the growth of each member of the family, being involved in each other's interests, and praying continually that God will allow the family to be a crucible for individual growth. The adventure of being a family or community is hard work, but the rewards are the richest to be found. It seems that the family is still truly the foundation of God's plan for peoplemaking.

NOTES

1. Carl Rogers, *On Personal Power* (New York: Delacorte Press, 1977).
2. Virginia Satir, *Peoplemaking* (Palo Alto, Calif.: Science and Behavior Books, 1972).
3. Burton White, *The First Three Years of Life* (Englewood Cliffs, N.J.: Prentice-Hall, 1975), p. 265.

10. Family Council

This chapter is about one method, one technique, for growing healthy people. It is especially for families with adolescents, although, as I have stated earlier, the best methods used to grow adolescent families are rooted in childhood. The structure of the method varies, but the intentions and spirit remain the same: it is the family council.

Because a family is a group of people who live together, they must communicate with some degree of effectiveness if their experience is to be a positive one. Making this happen sometimes requires the diligence and persistence of a general.

"How do you make any sense out of it?" asks one mother of three children, ages 6, 9, and 15. "Your 6-year-old is home most of the day and night. Your 9-year-old wants to be chauffeured all over town to various activities. Your 15-year-old is spending after-school time with groups of friends and has no time and little interest in doing anything with the family."

For Mom, it feels as if she has become a recreational director and taxi driver; for Dad, life is spent pushing to earn a living, juggling to find a little peace and quiet for himself, and at the same time straining to listen to the latest adventures of the other family members. For each child, the task often becomes playing the game, "How can I get what I want?"

Some family specialists are defining families as vital training centers where the basic transactions of life can best be rehearsed and solutions worked out. These laboratories for all ages are centers for experiments in problem solving and are—say some—at the heart of God's plan for us.

When the family is viewed as a caring community and not merely a hotel, the needs of all family members must be considered. If Mary needs to jog every morning at 5:30, John needs to be at Little League practice at 3:00, Bill has severe learning disabilities, Mom is going back to college, and Dad has been offered a new job in another city, the schedule gets very complicated. In fact, in every "laboratory" the ingredients are complex, and casual hit-or-miss communication will not be enough. If our aim really is to "grow people" and develop a healthy family community, a great deal of deliberate attention must be given to goals, plans, and consequences for family life.

The family council is a family management meeting. The family council functions to coordinate and facilitate the growth and development of each person. Thus, the family council is a family meeting with specific rules and regulations followed by all, but which can be changed. The best time to introduce an adolescent to a family council is at birth. From infancy, a child should feel that "in this family we do things together."

ASSUMPTIONS OF THE COUNCIL

- A family council allows for each family member to have a voice in deciding family rules.

- It provides the structure for an adolescent to air personal opinions and reasoning, and to receive serious feedback about his or her desires. All members of the family should have time to state their opinions and feelings, and should feel that they have been heard even if the final decision was not their first choice.
- The family council should be part of the family's mode of operation from the beginning. The rules made when the children are young, however, will differ from those made by families with older children. Adolescents need more power than younger children in decision making, and their contributions will be invaluable if they have learned how to work together for creative and effective decisions.
- Councils with younger children are used mainly for teaching; during adolescence, they are better used for communication, planning, and problem solving.

In her book *The Christian Mother*, Jackie Hertz stresses the importance of a family council:

> . . . it was the family council that first produced the kind of give-and-take discussion where the child feels no threat of being cut off or closed out or punished. . . . A circle of love is set up whereby the child gains the same kind of close group acceptance some can't find at home, so they seek it in a pot party or a kegger. . . . If we don't cement family values and love for them very, very early, our way out society will take its inevitable toll.[1]

A council is based on the belief that we can make better decisions and best help each other if we all work together. It also assumes that we are made to care and to be cared for, to bear each other's loads, to fulfill each other in responsible relationships. That kind of love is based on decision and commitment and not simply on warm feelings and self-satisfaction. If you want to call all the shots for the family, don't have a council; call a board meeting with yourself as president. Or call a press conference with yourself on the throne. If you call that kind of meeting a council, your hypocrisy will slowly oppress your subjects, and soon they will rebel out of bitterness. This is an almost predictable end-product, so weigh the risk. In the end you, as well as your subjects, will lose.

A council is not the only way to go. Other suggestions have been and will be made throughout the book. It is one technique you can use to accomplish your desired goals. However, for it to be an effective tool, you must use it correctly.

It must be appropriately designed and carefully executed. You must have your desired goals clearly in mind, and periodically evaluate them. A goal such as, "to help my teenager grow up" is too vague. Goals such as, "to understand money management," "to plan an unforgettable family vacation," "to work on age-related sex education," and "to help all members share and understand feelings" are specific, and lend themselves to creative planning and to checkpoints along the way that everyone can look at and meet.

A council also provides for flexibility in considering needs. This makes it an appropriate operation for family life from birth to death. Couples who work at meeting each other's needs before they have children will find it natural to include their baby when it arrives. The first three years of life provide vital learning opportunities. Then they will move on into the 4- to 9-year-old stage, ready to facilitate good judgment, use of money, and patterns for friendship in the development of their child. For the young adolescent, who needs to sense new power in the family and who needs to try out independence and to attempt self-support, a council provides a base for emotional expression and experimental control. It encourages older adolescents who need to pull up roots and move out on their own. Even for the young adult, single or married, trying to put together a career, the council can still function supportively. For the middle-aged adult seeking to live purposefully in between generations, and for the elderly person living out life with dignity, worth, and adventure, it is still a workable device for comfort and reflective observation. A well-run family council can become the workshop for a healthy performance by all family members. However, success is not automatic in the family any more than it is in a Broadway play. The skill in using this tool is gained through sensitive planning and continued practice.

WHAT IS A COUNCIL?

A family council is basically a set time, scheduled at the convenience of all members, when all family members can meet together for the explicit purpose of communicating and planning, and for evaluating that communication and planning. A family council differs radically from a business meeting. Remember that a family is a "community"; this means that the *process* of the encounter—or what happens to and between people—is as important as the task or the content of the meeting.

Don't be fooled by thinking that you can run a family council meeting the same way most company department meetings are run. The family's product is people. This is not the same as the packaged product of most companies. What are some of the differences between the usual department meeting and a family council?

- In a business, you are committed to a task and to a product; in the family, you are committed to caring for people.

- In a company, the basic need is for content; in a family, the important focus is on process.
- In a business, you meet only as often as is necessary to complete the task; in a family, there is high priority on just being together.
- In a business, decision-making is delegated to others to carry out; in a family, there is high commitment to work together and to be involved in the results of each member's decisions.
- There is very little or no involvement outside of the committee meeting with members of a company; in a family, there is endless involvement outside of the council between family members.

I like to think of a council as having two ingredients: (1) a contract; (2) a positive, friendly atmosphere where individual growth can take place.

A contract contains certain agreements made by all family members in answer to such questions as: What is the purpose of the council? What structure, policies, or rules should we use? What rules do we need to make it work? Who will be the leader of the council? What procedures will we use to reach a decision agreeable to all? A contract is an agreement between family members. It is always negotiable, changing as the family needs change.

This may sound complex, but it can be simplified a great deal. If too many areas are overlooked, however, the possibility exists for a stagnant, confusing, unproductive, or boring experience. The architects of a family council—usually the parents or parent—are much like the originators of any small group that comes together for mutual commitment. You will profit from knowing about group dynamics to obtain the most productive participation of each member of your family.

A contract is always open for negotiation, though it can be destructive to change it too often. Most families establish some working guidelines (norms), such as: any item is open for discussion; decision is by consensus; majority rule, or parents, have a deciding vote in case of a stalemate; each person is responsible for expressing his or her own opinions or feelings; meetings will be at a set time, for instance, each Sunday night after dinner for two hours. These guidelines help the meeting go smoothly and are changed as they prove to be impractical or no longer fit the intended purpose.

The purpose of the meeting can change, though the overall purpose of *communication, planning,* and *evaluation* usually stays the same. A family might decide to spend three sessions on sex education, planning a community service project, or just getting to know each other better. Or it may spend the time working on a family project or craft, reading a book, or even going to the zoo or to the soccer game. These specific purposes, suggested by individuals, need to be agreed upon by the others. They often provide a creative break from the usual council procedure, which works more intensely on the building of family.

The next chapter is an example of one family council's attempt to establish a working contract.

NOTES

1. Jackie Hertz, *The Christian Mother* (New York: Hawthorn Books, Inc., 1976), pp. 113, 114.

11. Family Council–How One Family Does It

The Martin family is made up of Dad, Mom, a 15-year-old daughter, and a 9-year-old son. They came for counseling because Mom was at her wits' end with Heather, their daughter.

Being affluent, the Martins live in a neighborhood where they are surrounded by young people with plenty of money. The parents in this area are successful because they have produced, and they encourage their young people to be productive. The high school has an excellent academic ranking nationally.

The school also has very clear-cut social groups that sanction certain behaviors if you belong to the group. The athletic crowd insists on athletic participation or loyal spectatorship to be a member of that group. The "freaks" insist on conformity to a distinctive kind of clothing and critical attitudes toward parents and other authorities. Also characteristic of this group is the fact that they "hang out" as part of their identity demon-

stration. Caught between these two groups are a great many
young people who need relationships but have no group to
belong to. For lack of anything more suitable, they attach
themselves to one of the two "in" groups. Because these boys
and girls are so eagerly reaching out, they will do almost anything the group says to do to gain approval.

Heather Martin found herself struggling for friendships and
approval from her peers; her rebellion toward her mother was
actually an attempt to be somebody on her own. Her mother,
however, took Heather's behavior personally and reacted with
hostility, anger, and finally depression.

When the family came in for counseling, they were in a
win-lose position. There was no way for everybody to win;
the lines had been drawn, and their positions in the family
were at stake. If Heather said she was going to her girlfriend's
house and ended up at a local party, naturally Mom found
out and felt it was a defiant act against her personally. If
Mom, in anger, grounded Heather or cut off her phone privileges, Heather took it as a sign that she was right all along:
her mother really did not understand her and was trying to
force her to be something other than herself.

Another dynamic was that Heather and Dad had a pretty
friendly relationship, and Dad became the middleman for
both Mom and Heather. It wasn't unusual for Dad to come
home and for Mom to unload the events of her day, followed
by Heather unloading the events of her day. He was caught
in between wanting to protect his wife and wanting to be
understanding to his daughter. Don, the 9-year-old son was
in many ways an ideal young man. He was held up frequently
before Heather as the example she should follow, which only
stirred up the waters between Heather and Don, who were
constantly trying to do each other in.

Though this is only one kind of power struggle, it represents the cold war going on in many families, where parents and the children are caught up in the great American tradition of winning or losing.

In the case of the Martins, if Heather hung out with the freaks, Heather won and Mom lost; and when Mom lost, Dad lost. If Heather came home late and was grounded, Heather lost and Mom won. When Dad was able to work out some kind of a compromise between Heather and Mom, Dad lost, because both Heather and Mom were trying to get Dad on their side, and any compromise is a sign that "you don't really love me." There was very little joy, freedom, and the deep emotional commitment that characterize a healthy, growing family.

Though the family had attempted a type of family council or family meeting in the past, it had always ended in chaos. Mom and Dad brought the ideas to the meeting; Heather was bored, resentful, and angry; and Don saw it as an opportunity to play the role of the good boy, which caused even more dissension in the family. It appeared to me that the family would benefit by some kind of structure for a family meeting or a council, and that someone from the outside was going to have to help them set it up.

Together we decided that the family would meet once a week in my office for the purpose of figuring out how each member of the family was going to survive in this atmosphere. I saw this as a good opportunity to teach the family about family councils and to model for them how I run a family council.

At our first meeting, we talked about and listed the personal desires for each family member. Some of these were vague; others very specific; some were individual, while others were family-oriented. Dad's goals ranged from providing a reasonable financial basis to enjoying family recreation and having individual dates with the children. Mom asked for peace and quiet in the evenings, some volunteer work in the community, a constructive relationship with her daughter, and management of the home. Heather wanted to be able to plan her own time without so much hassle, to be able to stay out later at night, and to begin to date. Don set goals to get good grades, to do better in athletics, and to do more with Dad. Once we had clearly stated these goals, I used them to teach the family a technique that is helpful in running a family meeting. It is called contracting.

CONTRACTING

Contracting is used to facilitate both individual and family growth. The family council is a time for family members to list their various desires and then to negotiate a reasonable plan for achieving these goals within the structure of the family. The family council is a time of give and take.

During contracting, it is not uncommon to hear, "I would be happy to extend your hours on Friday and Saturday night if you would study for three hours a day." To which there comes the reply, "It seems to me that three hours a day is a little more than is necessary. How about two and a half? And if my grades come up, could we talk about dropping it down to two hours?" And then the response, "That sounds fair enough. Let's go with that and see what happens."

For a family with a young person who is rapidly becoming an adult, there is a need for the adolescent to be given some power in family decisions. Contracting is one way to continue teaching an adolescent to take responsibility and to experience some authority in his or her decisions. For the first time in her life, Heather was aware that she had some say or some control over her own life. However, this did not come without her also taking responsibility and some potential consequences. Mom and Dad were willing to bend on her staying out later, providing Heather would keep up her part of the contract and study a certain number of hours.

It became apparent after four weeks of contracting that the family had initiated a new process of communication, and that this process carried some new responsibilities for everyone.

Since the old patterns were ingrained deeply, Heather's first attempt at studying and coming in on time was a total flop. When this happened, it became evident to her that the consequences established were her consequences. She had agreed that if she came in late, she would not be able to go out the following Friday and Saturday. Mom and Dad also felt the weight begin to lift from their shoulders as their role changed from policeman to arbitrator or negotiator. Heather also found that when she kept her end of the bargain, she received certain privileges. It was automatic because it was written down and agreed upon ahead of time. Heather and Mom and Dad began to work through some very painful experiences, which also made life more exciting and made them understand how very important it is for individuals to be responsible for their own actions.

It was not easy for Mom and Dad. Though they did not sacrifice any of their deeply held values, they were called upon to stretch themselves and to trust in some areas where there had been no trust previously. It was an uneasy matter of give and take, but it was a good learning experience.

In the case of the Martins, the results are still pending; but they do have a new method of communication, which takes into account the needs of all of the family members. The family council has changed from a session of intense negotiation, fraught with high degrees of hostility and anger, to a workable session for family communication. For the most part, power struggles are absent as the family members try to work out their disagreements in an atmosphere of respect.

STYLES OF FAMILY LEADERSHIP

Families are communities, and, like any other small group, they require leadership. Leadership styles vary, but they tend to fall within four general categories: autocratic leadership, authoritarian leadership, democratic leadership, and laissez-faire leadership. John Conger states that the style of leadership most conducive to adolescent growth and development is a democratic style where the parents hold final authority.[1] Let's define these four styles of leadership briefly to put this statement into focus.

In an *autocratic* style of leadership, the leader is responsible for every function of the group, and many of the functions are actually performed by the leader. All responsibility and authority lies with the leader. This style of leadership says, "I'll tell you what to do, and you do it."

Under *authoritarian* leadership, the leader appoints group members to perform certain functions. Authority still lies with the leader, but the functions of the group are spread around at the leader's direction, and the group members perform these functions. This differs from autocratic leadership in that the leader does not perform all of the functions of the group. There are two subgroupings under the authoritarian leadership style: paternalistic and personalistic style.

In the *paternalistic-authoritarian* group, the leader is a "father figure," recognized as the person with all wisdom and knowledge on any subject. When the group exhausts itself in discussion, it then turns to the "father figure" for the answer to the problem. There can be discussion among the members, but the final authority rests in the leader, who is viewed as the one with the answers.

In a *personalistic-authoritarian* group, the leader is an individual with a great deal of charisma. People in the group will do anything for the leader because of his or her strength of personality. As in the paternalistic group, this leader decides what the group needs to do and then asks or appoints members of the group to do the task. It is still the leader who has full authority, however.

Under the *democratic* style of leadership, decisions are made by concensus. Usually this group will form around a certain task to be done, and the leader facilitates the completion of that task. The leader's responsibility is to convene the group, to prepare the agenda, and to lead the group toward the goal of completing the task. In a democratic group, the members of the group are the decision makers; they decide who performs what functions. The leader is seen as an active participant in the group, but the authority lies in the hands of the group itself.

In the fourth leadership style—*laissez-faire*—the leader does little more than convene the group, giving it no direction from that point on. Often the leader is not a participant in the group, but is seen as someone outside the group.

From what we know about groups, it is safe to say that different types of groups are best for accomplishing different purposes. In a crisis situation, it may be very appropriate for someone to be an autocratic/authoritarian leader, taking complete charge of the situation and telling people what to do and how to do it. Thus, autocratic groups function best when there is a defined task to be accomplished and an expert is on the scene to direct people in accomplishing that task. The autocratic style of leadership is generally not best for a family. Though a parent may find that doing all of the family functions personally seems quick and efficient, it often results in children who are bitter and unskilled, and who lack good judgment. These children will grow up without having had the opportunity of venturing out and taking some risks in living. Not having experienced trust from their parents, they don't expect others to trust them either.

The authoritarian style of leadership seems to be beneficial for childhood years, especially if the parents are good authorities. Since the parents have had considerable experience in living and should have accumulated a certain amount of wisdom, they should be able to set some guidelines and provide some structure for the family unit. In this kind of structure, each child can feel a certain sense of security in knowing that the parents have his or her best interests at heart. The dangers of being a strictly authoritarian leader in the family rear their ugly heads as the child approaches preadolesence. There is a time in a young person's life when the parent takes an additional risk in order to help the young person become independent. These risks must be intelligently calculated, and the authoritarian style of leadership must change toward the democratic style, where all the evidence is gathered but parents hold the final vote. For example, a parent may feel that the young person is making an unwise judgment but could most likely learn from the experience. In this case, the parent might say, "I really don't agree fully with what you're intending to do, but I'll go along with it. Let's talk it over a little more and see how I might be of help to you in what you are proposing to do."

This shift in the style of family leadership needs to begin somewhere around the preadolescent stage of development. Then as the young person gains more experience, the move is naturally made to more of a democratic style of leadership, where the young person is encouraged to be responsible and self-supportive. Some parents realize, however, that some young people need much more support than others because of continuing poor judgment. Unfortunately, chronological age doesn't absolutely correlate with good judgment. There are 18-year-olds who are at an 11- and 12-year-old maturity level when it comes to judgment.

Being a parent is the highest of the arts, and the most effective style of government used within the family is always open for reevaluation.

There is no indication that a laissez-faire style is ever appropriate for a family. It seems to encourage loose families and self-centered concerns within the family. A characteristic statement I often hear from young people is, "Nobody really cares about me. I sort of just do my own thing." Laissez-faire leadership seems to be unproductive, even destructive, in family situations.

What does all this say about a family council? In most cases, a family is a small group with a task to accomplish. The style of leadership of that group is extremely important and will vary with the age of the family members. The convener of a family council (usually the parent, especially in families with young children) will probably get the best results when the group is run democratically. Family members are individuals, and they feel that they are important. They feel they have something to offer the family, they feel ownership in the family, they feel cared for and know how to care for each other. The democratic style allows each family member the chance to contribute to the council and to receive guidance from it.

In summary, a family is a small group, and the style of leadership within the family will have a bearing on each individual's growth and development, just as it does in any other group.

NOTES

1. John Conger, "Current Issues in Adolescent Development" in Supplement 1334 to *Masters Lectures on Developmental Psychology* (Journal Supplement Abstract Service of the American Psychological Association).

12. Troubled Families: What Are the Signs?

One way of discovering whether your family is troubled or nurturing, is to ask these three questions suggested by Virginia Satir in her book, *Peoplemaking:*

- Does it feel good to you to live in your family right now?
- Do you feel you are living with friends, people you like and trust, and who like and trust you?
- Is it fun and exciting to be a member of your family?

"If you can answer 'yes' to those three questions," says Satir, "I am certain you live in what I call a nurturing family. If you answer 'no' or 'not often,' you probably live in a family that is more or less troubled."[1]

TODAY'S TROUBLED FAMILIES

A number of sources are suggesting that families today are troubled. *U.S. News and World Report* posed the question,

"Can the American family survive today's shocks?"[2] The article suggests we are in a turbulent era of experimentation and change for the American family. Implications of this family trouble are all around us:

- Divorce rates are rising, even among older Americans.
- There is a marked increase in extramarital affairs, especially among women.
- More that 450,000 youngsters are living with their divorced or separated fathers.
- One million young Americans, most of them middle class, run away from home each year.
- Suicide is now the second leading cause of death for young Americans between ages 18 and 24.
- By age 17, one out of ten American women—married or unmarried—is a mother, despite the widening availability of birth-control measures.
- One out of nine youths appears in juvenile court by age 18.
- Drug abuse and alcoholism are serious public-health problems among teenagers.

Urie Bronfenbrenner, Cornell University Professor of Human Development and Psychology, also notes that the American family is in trouble. He says: "The family is falling apart. There is a lot of evidence to substantiate this. Since World War II the extended family of several generations, with all its relatives, has practically disappeared in this country. Even the small nuclear family of mother, father and kids is in decline. . . . What's destroying the family isn't the family itself but the indifference of the rest of society. The family takes a low priority."[3]

We are told by Bronfenbrenner that 6 percent of today's children have no parent at home during the day; that one-sixth are living in single-parent families; and that one-third of all women who have children under age 3 are working. Bronfenbrenner asks,

> . . . Who is caring for American's children? The answer is disturbing. Fewer and fewer parents are doing their job of caring for children. . . .
> Increasing numbers of children are coming home to empty houses. If there's any reliable predictor of trouble, it probably begins with children coming home to an empty house, whether the problem is reading difficulties, truancy, dropping out, drug addiction, or childhood depression.[4]

I am convinced that the family is an important key to an individual's happiness. It was established by God (Genesis 1, 2) to provide a nurturing atmosphere for all its members. Family living can be an exciting adventure of constructive experiences of acceptance, confidence, and well-being; or it can be full of destructive experiences of rejection, fear, and feelings of worthlessness. Before we go any further it is well worth deciding whether your family is troubled or nurturing, and finding out what you can do about it if it is troubled. Let's look for clues.

THREE QUESTIONS

Question 1: *Does it feel good to you to live in your family right now? How does it feel—lonely, happy, exciting, insecure, tense, ecstatic, joyful, trusting, hurt, frustrating, secure, interesting, painful?* (This question assumes that you are able to identify your feelings accurately.)

Your family didn't give you feelings; God "built" you to feel. People and situations only stimulate your feelings. You do the feeling. Your entire life has been filled with feelings; and your family has helped teach you what to do with all of these feelings, how to act them out. Your family, in this sense, has been a laboratory, a place to find out what actions are OK and what actions are not OK.

Some families know the importance of teaching their members that feelings are OK and that it is important to express them. These children are taught to listen closely to their feelings and to view them as friends. They are able to use their feelings as guides in making decisions to act. In these cases, the children pursue the task of developing a wide range of feelings. Life becomes an adventure of "tuning in" and listening to this marvelous God-given channel of communication.

Because these children have been taught to feel, they often experience family as good, a place where it is safe to try out different actions. I am not saying that all their feelings will be pleasant. We know only too well that many feelings are disturbing, frightening, or sad. But the channels for feeling are open; the children are alive, tracking, hearing God; and it feels good to them to live in their family right now.

Other families, whether they mean to or not, teach their members that feelings cannot be trusted; feelings are suspect, changeable, and can get you into lots of trouble if you follow them. These family members appear guarded, skeptical, and tightly rational. They seem not to feel at all. Moments of joy and of disappointment produce the same calm exterior. Life appears serious and task-oriented. It may be superficially pleasant or exasperatingly indifferent.

Children in this kind of family grow up learning that feelings are enemies. They try hard not to show feelings; they may even succeed in shutting down their emotional system so that they actually don't feel much. Sooner or later, however, feelings will insist on being felt; they cannot be disregarded and held down forever.

People who have not made friends with their feelings, or

who have been taught in their families that feelings are dangerous, may not feel very good about living in the family. They
may feel fine today, but tomorrow is uncertain and may bring
conflict, anger, resentment, dread, depression, and self-disgust.
If they have not learned to listen to these feelings as God-
given, but see them as enemies out to destroy them, they
will want to escape from them. They may resort to drugs or
unusual defenses to help them cope. In doing this, they miss
out on a wide sweep of life.

Question 2: *Do you feel you are living with friends, people
you like and trust, and who like you and trust you?*

Have you ever felt not liked or not trusted? Often in therapy
I hear, "Dad doesn't trust me. He won't let me do anything.
Everything is regulated by his policies and rules. He's scared
to death that I'm going to ruin his reputation in town. He
doesn't seem to realize that I'm 16 now and can make some
decisions."

And from Dad I hear, "My daughter doesn't like me. I
give her a roof over her head, food, and security. She treats
me like a doormat. All I get is hostile looks, snide remarks,
sarcasm, and putdowns. She doesn't ever bother to introduce
me to her friends. She doesn't want a Dad, she wants a never-
ending bank account."

Being trusted and feeling liked are basic to personal growth
no matter how old we are. A person who is trusted and liked
feels special and important. From the earliest assignments
to "make your bed and pick up your toys," to the everyday
expectations of adulthood to "be home at six," "get the kids
in bed by eight," and "call Mr. Jones about the board meeting," trust helps us like ourselves.

Friends are people we trust. They don't use us for their
own gain. They love us for no good reason at all. We look
forward to being with them; they make us feel important.

The aphorism, "the family is the place that when you go there they have to take you in," expresses one aspect of the importance of family. A nurturing family is committed to the growth of its members. It means instant friends, a community of people deeply in love with every part of us.

Of course, not all families are nurturing; not all families are friends committed to each other and involved in each other's lives. Many families are troubled. Their relationships are governed by fear—of control, exploitation, and manipulation.

Some parents control their children with the fear of punishment. In fact, fear can control any one of us. Children fear physical punishment. Adolescents fear restriction. Adults fear loss of sexual privileges, physical abuse, or emotional harrassment. Control by punishment is effective but emotionally costly. The results are usually deep bitterness, resentment, loneliness, inability to trust, depression, feelings of worthlessness and alienation, and a negative, guarded approach to life.

Exploitation means that we intentionally use people in a way that hurts them personally. The results are deep hurt and tendency to trust no one. Manipulation, another destructive attempt at family relations, ranges from continual bribes, such as candy and toys, to gifts that replace personal involvement, to promises that the future will be different if the person "puts up with" the now. Such manipulation can cause family members to become selfish and thing-oriented, bitter and hopeless, or to display subtle tendencies of any of these. Control, exploitation, and manipulation are all destructive motives, that can slowly erode a person's self-worth.

By the time manipulated children become teenagers, manipulation has become an expected way of life. They want what they want: Do I have enough things, the right things, and does everybody know it? This attitude covers up insecurity;

the "Am I in?" question frequently nags manipulated teenagers, who wonder if anybody truly cares for them.

I sat with 15-year-old Christi and her mother as the girl stated boldly in a tone suggesting that any idiot would agree, "My goal is to be rich, to have a huge house, lots of clothes, a tennis court and beautiful, fancy cars. And I'm going to do it. That's what I want, and that's when I'll be happy."

Christi's attitude gives her away. People need people to love and care for them if they are to be fulfilled and happy. The odds are high that Christi is grasping for a false sense of security and that her life will be dominated by a constant strategy of manipulating others for her own selfish purposes.

Guard against manipulation as a technique for raising your children. Instead of trying to make your child into something, ask yourself what type of person you want your child to become, then be that type of person yourself. A model is a powerful teacher. Act out your desires for your children and teenagers and more than likely they will absorb your qualities—even more than you would ever think. Above all, be trustworthy.

Question 3: *Is it fun and exciting to be a member of your family?*

Nurturing families have fun. It's exciting to be in a family where people feel open and are spontaneous in expressing their feelings. Here family members are for each other; they laugh with each other, like being together, are free to play with each other, are proud of each others' success, and are quick to support each other when life caves in.

In many families, having fun is not acceptable. Life is serious business and, above all, people must be successful. Intense feelings of joy, happiness, pleasure, or excitement produce guilt, because family members have learned that these feelings are wrong. They think that people who have "too much fun"

are not serious about life. They have to focus on the importance of the task, the value of putting "their nose to the
grindstone" and making every minute count, to the exclusion
of enjoyment.

Families in which fun and excitement produce guilt are
usually families who have grown up with task-oriented parents,
who never learned to enjoy themselves. It is not fun to live
in these families because too much guilt is emotionally painful.
As many of us have learned, too much guilt is a sign of trouble,
while guilt which helps us develop better relationships and
function more effectively is truly helpful.

There is frequently an air of optimism in families that have
fun, an optimism related to reality. Problems are not overlooked or denied; they are faced creatively as growth and
learning opportunities, with energy generated by feelings. In
fact, problem solving often becomes a family effort that provides an excitement all its own.

When our children were 5 and 6 years old, Judy and I
realized our desire for total family involvement in home main-
tenance. We decided to approach this task with an air of
optimism by calling a family meeting. Both Jeff and Jennifer
responded to the challenge and suggested a division of labor
among the four of us. We set up charts for the children
listing a combination of their ideas and ours. Discussing the
idea as a family helped Jeff and Jennifer realize their responsibility in planning and in sharing the load, and in knowing
that our house belongs to all of us and we all are responsible
for its upkeep.

One day, after several weeks of charting the results of our
labors, I pointed out to Jeff that he seemed to be slipping
in the area of personal grooming. He reacted with a number
of excuses, telling me how it was difficult to be called "down"
for his behavior "all the time." Then he cocked his head

slightly to the right and said, "Anyway, where is your chart?" He had called my attention to the lack of involvement by Judy and me in this visible expression of mutual accountability. He added that he didn't necessarily want us to have charts, but he did want to know how we spent our time. Jeff and I talked it over, and as I think back, maybe a chart for Mom and Dad would have been a good idea. He was wondering if the arrangement was fair, since I was not working on the same basis he was.

Families who have fun also seem to have plenty of energy for attacking problems. There is a spirit of cooperation buoyed up by challenge, eagerness, and excitement. In addition, there is an air of expectancy, a harmony that multiplies the strength of the family rather than depleting it. Excitement is felt even when the family faces serious loss.

In summary, ask yourself:

- Is each of our family members encouraged to feel all of his or her feelings and to express them?
- Do the members of our family like each other, and is there a high level of trust among our family members?
- Is fun considered each time our family plans activities?
- Do we plan enough recreation in our family schedules?
- Are we as parents spontaneous in expressing our feelings, and do we model enjoyment and enthusiasm in our family?

How are you doing so far? Remember, answers of "no" or "not often" may be clues that describe a family more troubled than nurturing. Troubled families often have more than their share of the following:

- Relationships are governed by control, exploitation, and manipulation.

- Parents tell their children one thing, but don't do it themselves.
- Family rules are handed down by the parents, rigid and nonnegotiable, with no chance for suggesting or questioning by the children.
- Learning is motivated more by punishment than by reinforcement.
- Family members act separately, with very little time shared with the family.

My hope for you as you complete this chapter is that you will be able to feel as though a buoyant outrigger has been affixed to your family ship—not that you're going to sink. Trouble is a part of life and can be a step toward success. Most things that cause families to be troubled are learned after birth. That means they can be unlearned. New ways of dealing with life can be learned in their place.

Virginia Satir gives three pointers in how to make this happen:

- "First, you need to recognize that your family *is* a troubled family.
- "Second, you need to have some hope that things can be different.
- "Third, you need to take some action to start the changing process."[5]

When you clearly see yourself and your family as troubled, please don't feel guilty—IF you also are willing to work at the problems you see. Undoubtedly, much of the pain you are experiencing occurs because you've not known how to prevent or change that pain. Many people grow up without any know-how in what we call human or personal skills. If this is true in your case, take heart. You don't have to remain a cripple in this area. What you need to do is develop an eagerness to change, and a willingness to take the necessary action to start changing.

NOTES

1. Virginia Satir, *Peoplemaking* (Palo Alto, Calif.: Science and Behavior Books, 1972), p. 9.
2. *U.S. News and World Report,* "The American Family: Can It Survive Today's Shocks?" October 27, 1975, pp. 30–46.
3. Urie Bronfenbrenner, "Nobody Home: The Erosion of the American Family," *Psychology Today,* May, 1977, p. 41.
4. Bronfenbrenner, p. 41.
5. Satir, p. 19.

13. Teenage Runaways

WHERE DID WE GO WRONG?

When Julie's parents and I finally found 15-year-old Julie, she was "wasted" after three months on the street. She had run away from her middle-class family, where all the material goods she could use had provided a "good life." We found her in a low-cost apartment, living with other young people, all of whom were trying to make it on their own.

She squinted at us through eyes that were bloodshot and yellowed from drug abuse and no sleep. Her face was drawn, her mind incoherent and "spacey." What we did not know was that she had recently had her first abortion. She was reluctant to talk with us, but she did. That talk started a friendship that was to last for more than two years. Later it became apparent that though Julie's family had designated her as the problem, the problem actually was a family problem. And while finding her ended one search, it also began another—the search for a meaningful family.

Julie's mother knew her daughter was in town, but her persistent efforts to get Julie to come home met with constant resistance and hostility. As a last straw, the mother contacted me. Extremely frustrated, she asked through her tears, "What happened? Where did we go wrong? What do we do now?"

While the steps in solving the problem looked easy, working it out was going to be much more difficult. The steps were these: (1) find Julie; (2) talk about the problem; (3) work on a solution; (4) make sure it doesn't happen again.

We found Julie and I persuaded her to talk with me. Convincing her, however, that she and I should talk with her parents was another story. When we met with them, it took hours of yelling, name calling, blaming, and walking out before we were able to identify the real problems. Misinterpretation, misunderstanding, and deep hurt had all been a part of living together, and it all had to surface. It was obvious that permanent healing would take time for Julie and her mom and dad.

One statistic flashed through my mind at that meeting. It has been estimated that 60 percent of runaway young people return home within four weeks.[1] This figure is misleading and can leave parents with a "Little Bo Peep" philosophy— "leave them alone and they'll come home." The main question, however, is, "To what are they returning?" *My conviction is that deep inside all of us is the need and desire for the loving atmosphere of a family,* and if children don't find it at home, a natural instinct to be cared for will drive them to seek it elsewhere—religious cults, prostitution, precipitous marriage, and so on. On the other hand, I also know that many families are destructive, and even I do not want to send young people back into a family that is systematically shaping destruction. The price is too great.

Statistics do not tell the story on runaways. The complexity of legal definitions, police policies on dealing with runaways, and the circumstances surrounding each individual situation make one wonder what the statistics are saying. Christine Chapman, author of *America's Runaways,* reports:

> Statistics released in 1974 by the University of Michigan's Institute for Social Research suggested that the number of runaways was lower than we had believed and that the majority stayed close to home and returned soon after the episode. The uncertainty of the runaway population continues. A statistician from the Department of Health, Education, and Welfare estimated it at three or four million annually! The truth was not to be found in official statistics.[2]

By running away, Julie had "freed" herself to an unending prison without walls. She had run away *from* something, but had nothing better to run *to.* So she arrived quickly at what was available—more drugs, exploitation, and abuse. And things got worse.

COMBATTING ALIENATION

National statistics indicate that one million young people leave home under stress every year.[3] Though the media do not focus on the problem as much as they did in the late 1960s, in my opinion, the problem is still very much with us and speaks to the inadequacy of our families. Many of these young people are getting away from a "hot situation," and there needs to be some cooling off. Their running away is one way of handling pressure; but often it is more of an escape than a solution.

The goals of the Dale House Project are: (1) to train Christians in social action; that is, how to intervene effectively in this crisis we call "runaway"; (2) to provide food, shelter, and counseling for young people needing help; (3) to reunite runaway young people with their families; and (4) to provide effective intervention with families in crisis, as well as ongoing counseling, referral to local community agencies, and a supportive community for continual contact. Our primary goal, stated briefly, is to help meet the spiritual, psychological, physical, and intellectual needs of alienated young people and their families, within the context of a caring Christian community. Because Julie did not want to return home, and because she was "burnt out" on the street, she chose to come to the Dale House. It was a compromise to see if something could be worked out. The counselor who first talked with her described her as hostile, angry, self-destructive, and filled with a sense of worthlessness and self-hate. As with anyone entering the project, the first step was to build trust. Our staff took a few days to get to know Julie, start a relationship, and try to build some trust. She was on drugs, but it was evident that drugs were not the real problem. She was out of tune with her family and with society. She had deep personal fears of failing and not being able to make it anywhere. For her, drugs, sexual involvement, and running away were ways of coping with those fears. Even though she was experiencing intense pleasure, she knew that the price she was paying was beginning to take its toll.

Once Julie moved in with us at Dale House, we could attempt to be a family to her and help her find meaning in life. She is like many of the three hundred young people who come to the project each year because they aren't making it with their own families.

During my five years at the Dale House project, I have counseled with many parents and young people caught in the midst of a runaway problem. In the dimly lit rooms of "crash" houses; during an anxious, frustrating, long-distance telephone call; or in the simply furnished office of a walk-in clinic, I have heard many reasons given for running away:

It was all I could do to leave, and I just couldn't face my parents, but I'll never go back.

I told them that I would go, but they didn't believe me. Anyway, I split, and I think they'll probably never understand.

A lot of my friends were leaving, and I just thought it would be kind of fun.

Mom and Dad were constantly destroying each other, and I couldn't stand it any longer.

I wanna see if I can make it on my own.

My dad raped me.

Parents say:

Where have we failed?

That's typical of the way she tried to solve her problems.

I guess they'll have to learn the hard way.

The kid never had any sense.

It was that crowd of kids he started running around with.

It's evident to me that running away is an attempt to solve a problem. The problem is alienation—strong feelings of separation or rejection that explode inside, and "I have to run." Alienation is a family problem that usually brews for years. A closer look often reveals that, in running away, the teenager is simply doing what the parents have been doing for years.

Adult runaways are more difficult to spot. They cover for their absence in socially acceptable ways, and often no one says the obvious—"Hey, I notice you're not home much," or "Your kids are always at my house." Running away for adults can take the form of:

- Working long hours to assure self-worth.
- Taking excessive steps to "get away from it all," such as drinking or sleeping.
- Staying together "for the sake of the children."
- Husbands and wives ignoring each other or sarcastically cutting each other down.
- Parents creating families with no emotion—systematically bankrupting their families of emotion until members of the family can no longer feel.
- Surrounding themselves with people and activities to avoid time for in-depth communication.

Destructive consequences of this adult "running away" are:

- Demanding better performance from both children and spouse rather than paying attention to their feelings.
- A lifestyle of side-stepping or ignoring conflict.
- Teaching children that friendship consists of casual superficial loyalties.
- A surface generosity that operates on the basis of personal convenience.
- Insensitivity to people's needs and an accumulation of selfish desires.
- Lack of a human "laboratory" or dynamic family where valuable skills of relationship are developed.

KINDS OF RUNAWAYS

My experience suggests that teenagers who run away fit into one of three categories: the runaway, the throwaway, or the just-plain-bored.

The *runaway* is running from a situation he or she can no longer tolerate. Conflict is so great that members of the family can hardly stand each other. Feeble attempts may be made to "get through," but there is no resolution. The pressure builds until the young person finally leaves home.

Another type of runaway is the young person who lives two lives. One pleases the parents, but a second, secret, life violates what the parents want. Parents become suspicious and begin to ask questions. It becomes more and more difficult to remember what excuse was given. The young person fears that the parents will "find out" and leaves home before the "lid blows."

The *throwaway* was usually rejected as a child. During adolescence, the rejection becomes more open and blatant, involving, for example, belittling, labeling, sarcasm, and unfavorable comparison with other children. To escape, the young person may start drifting; he or she leaves home with no resistance or is told to leave home for the sake of the family. The throwaway is told never to come home and never to get in touch with the family again. In fact, the throwaway is a family reject.

I've worked with too many throwaway adolescents. The message I hear from the parents is a clear, "I don't like the kid; they deserve what they get; don't bother me about it; they're on their own." The throwaway is difficult to work with because of expense. No one wants throwaways—they can't hold a job, they have no social graces, and even the simplest skills of relating are absent. They need food, shelter, and concentrated learning over a period of time. In short, they need a family. This costs money, and the results are slow. Community agencies, churches, and corporations generally will help anyone but the throwaway, yet this young person will bleed a community to death living on the street.

Finally, there is the *just-plain-bored*. The message I hear from them is, "No big conflict. My parents and I just agreed that home was sort of a 'place to land' for all of us, so I decided to do what everyone else is doing—drift. I really get into looking at people and seeing what's happening in other parts of the country." These young people are difficult to help because they don't want help. They stay one or two nights at Dale House and then move on. After two or three years of following drifters, however, I see bland, apathetic, superficial young people. Some of them are committed to nothing and desperate for love. This category of runaways is possibly the most frustrating to work with.

I am concerned for the runaway because the consequences of running away are usually much greater than expected. Life on the street, which at first seemed to be freeing, suddenly becomes an unrelenting steel trap. It can dramatically alter an unsuspecting young person's life. I have seen too many 14- and 15-year-olds completely at the mercy of drugs, sex, and the exploitation of junkies. For most of them, the road to maturity will be blocked with mistrust, hostility, abuse, and a quest for immediate gratification. And, for many of them, each day tips the balance of bondage and freedom more toward bondage. Each day the promised freedom becomes more bogged down in a drug habit or a sexual pattern that produces money for survival. Soon they are "locked in."

THE MODERN PRODIGAL SON

In the narrative of the prodigal son (Luke 15:22), the younger son decides to take his share of the inheritance and leave home. He gathers everything together, goes on a journey, and squanders his estate with loose living. He then attaches himself to a citizen of that country and things get worse.

I have seen many adolescents leave home with their "estate." The pinch of life on the street presents a new reality that, combined with pride and the intensity of difficulties at home, makes it hard to ask for help; and things get worse. Occasionally, they or their parents come to their senses—find themselves, and realize that, in running away, they have not left their problems, nor have their problems left them.

Initially, the prodigal son felt he could do better on his own. To him, freedom was getting away from the family. Soon, however, he was in bondage, a slave to survival and to his boss. Likewise, the young person seeking freedom on the street can almost overnight become a slave to survival, bitterness, drugs, self-centeredness, and insecurity. The pride that drove him or her from home becomes a slave-driver on the street.

Parents also become slaves to control or restrictions as a method of keeping peace in the family. Even after the young person has run away, parents usually refuse to admit any wrong. They continue to deny their part and to realize that most crises are two-sided.

THE RUNAWAY CRISIS

Is there any help for a family in a runaway crisis? Here are some clues that a crisis is developing, along with steps that can be helpful in resolving a crisis. Parents should be aware of both.

Stages of a Developing Crisis

Stage 1: There is a vague awareness that something is changing in the normal family order; for example, hints of child's rebellion, or parents "tightening up."

Bob had begun running around with a group of kids his family found undesirable. His grades began dropping, he radically changed his clothing style, and his interest in doing family things vanished. Both Bob and his parents knew something was happening, but they said nothing. There was no resolution of these conflicts, and the family moved into Stage 2.

Stage 2: Some conscious, unorganized attempt is made to deal with the conflict. Bob was confronted by his parents about his possible use of drugs and a suspicion of "immoral" behavior. He denied any involvement, though his parents felt there was adequate evidence to implicate him. Bob was restricted with early hours and guidelines as to whom his friends could be. Subsequently, a number of his friends mentioned seeing him "high" at parties. This news got back to his parents, but they didn't know what to do except to restrict him further. When he questioned the fairness of the restriction, he was told it was for his own good. Resolution did not occur, and the family moved into Stage 3.

Stage 3: Behavior becomes more blatant and reactionary. Outside people are sometimes brought in to aid in a solution.

Bob's parents engaged the services of a psychologist to work things out. Bob was resistant and suspicious of anyone his parents would choose. He participated in sessions for a while to "get his parents off his back." Then Bob got several of his friends to talk with his parents to convince them that nothing was wrong.

Results of both efforts were similar: Bob was not going to listen to any "shrink" on his parent's side; and the parents were not about to listen to a bunch of "freaks."

These attempts only widened the gap, encouraging additional resistance and rebellion with no resolution. The family moved into Stage 4—crisis!

Stage 4: When no resolution is achieved, parents often become openly aggressive and controlling with demands and threats, and the young person openly and defiantly rebels.

Bob's parents began meticulously observing his actions, belittling him, and confronting him with threats of police involvement and institutionalization if he didn't "shape up." He stayed away more, talked openly about his drug involvement, and finally left home.

The family was in crisis.

Resolving a Crisis

In cases of family crisis, outside intervention is needed. Emotions are raw and touchy, misunderstanding is rampant, and blame is leveled on all sides; hurt is deep, and steps to numb that hurt have already been clumsily taken. At this point, it becomes extremely painful to reopen wounds that have been scabbed over through escape. The skill of an outside person is necessary if healing is to take place.

Crisis is actually an opportunity for healing to begin. The healing will take time and hard work; it is naive to think that a crisis that has been building for years can be resolved in a week. Healthy resolution may take years, but we are dealing with a lifetime; and once resolutions are started, the excitement of working things out becomes deeply meaningful to the entire family. The urgent need is for intervention to solve the immediate crisis, and then for a long-range plan of family work.

Step 1: Finding an arbitrator agreeable to the family members. Since lack of trust is operating and each person feels abused by the other, the person chosen to help with the healing process must be agreeable to all sides. The arbitrator can be a trusted, sensitive neighbor, a teacher, or a friend. However, do not overlook the fact that a skilled professional trained in dealing with these situations may be your best bet. Agreement by all will represent a mutual commitment to work on the problem. This is important, as it sets a pattern of commitment for the future. If there is too much disagreement, change arbitrators and find one who is acceptable to all sides. Do not compromise competence, however, except as a last resort.

Step 2: Talking out the problem. A sensitive arbitrator will begin to explore the problem and identify each person's part. As this is accomplished, understanding will begin; things will begin to fit together. This step will take time and energy, but, if done properly, it will provide an adequate foundation for the family work of Step 3.

Step 3: Commitment to a plan. Once understanding has begun and the crisis is resolved, plans must be initiated to work through the problem. A skilled arbitrator will (1) draw out from each family member suggestions to assist in solving the problem; (2) help the family select a concrete plan of action; (3) gain commitment from each member to a plan; (4) provide the tools needed to implement the plan; and (5) establish an evaluation procedure to measure success or failure.

Step 4: Develop a family strategy *without* an arbitrator. The goals of arbitration are to resolve crisis, initiate solutions, and equip a family with tools so they can work out their own growth. Thus, an arbitrator can withdraw as he teaches the family new skills for relating on their own. After several sessions, the resolution should be in process, with each person using the new skills effectively.

Crisis can be the opportunity to grow, and the sooner it is identified and worked with, the greater the chances are for constructive change. Crisis is also short-lived—up to about six weeks. If there is no active intervention, crisis will resolve itself by implementing patterns of alienation and escape.

Therefore, if the crisis involves a runaway, do not assume that the problem is solved when the runaway returns home. Only the symptom is gone. Working through the problem is just beginning. If healing is to take place, that work will take sacrifice and commitment from all family members.

Unfortunately, I have seen families begin counseling, only to have Mom or Dad not show up, cancel most appointments at the last minute, or send the young person off alone to get "straightened out." For these families, the sacrifice is too great and their commitment to each other too shallow. They are continuing in their previous pattern of relating, and the crisis will be repeated.

INGREDIENTS OF A HEALTHY FAMILY

What does a healthy working family look like? We turn to Luke 15 to find some clues for parents. This family has the following ingredients: (1) an atmosphere where growth is encouraged; (2) sensitive parents living openly in relationships of caring; (3) parents willing to be there when help and guidance are needed; and (4) parents who realize that the family is a "factory" working to make people.

The father in the story demonstrates the first ingredient of a healthy family—*an atmosphere where growth is encouraged.* The father desires true independence for his son, and, with some fear, assists him in exercising his choice to leave. He feels that his son will learn only by being on his own and experiencing life; only then will he know what it means to be independent and self-supportive. This is not true for all adolescents or runaways.

The second ingredient of a healthy family is *parent sensitivity* that operates in a close relationship of caring. Sensitivity starts with a commitment by the parent to help learning take place. Leaving home is not the solution for all problems; in the case of the prodigal son, however, it works. Evidently the father was willing to risk that his son might not make good decisions, knowing full well that he might not "get his head together."

The father knew he had to allow his son a chance to make decisions on his own, and to suffer the consequences of those decisions. He was also *willing to be there* when help, guidance, or intervention was needed. This third ingredient is important in the changing role of the parent. Parents must be available but not in control as before. They must be willing to forgive, guide, and help in any way. There will be many unexpected detours along the way. These must be met with an expectation of growth, an atmosphere of sensitive guidance, and the certainty of someone being there.

Some young people run away from home emotionally rather than physically. This is true of the older brother in Luke 15. This brother had never gone away from home; he was faithful and obedient, and was promised the father's inheritance.

However, he, too, was lost—lost in the performance of being the oldest son. "I performed for you for years, have I done this for nothing?" (Luke 15:29). The father, being sensitive, hears this correctly as a cry for help. It is a reminder to parents that the nice, predictable, obedient child is sometimes very lost and needs an atmosphere for growth, sensitivity, and someone being there as much as the runaway does. It is easy for parents to overlook the "good" child.

Parents, it is urgent to recognize that family work is never over. Just when one crisis is resolved and the celebration is in full swing, there is another cry for help. The parents attend to it immediately, and the work of family goes on. This is normal for family life. The family is a human laboratory where lives are constantly in process, growing and changing. Sometimes this atmosphere will be relaxing, affirming, and fulfilling; at other times, it will be intensely demanding, uncomfortable, and emotionally draining. When done effectively, the process of family provides the ingredients that fulfill the primary objectives of our creation—learning to love ourselves and our "neighbor." God created us, and he is the fulfillment of our deepest longings, a fulfillment worked out in interaction with those who are significant to us. Running away provides one more opportunity to put into action those family ingredients that will bring fulfillment and healing at the deepest level.

NOTES

1. Christine Chapman, *America's Runaways* (New York: William Morrow and Company, Inc., 1976), pg. 32.
2. Ibid.
3. B. Bayh, in "Runaway Youth," Hearings before the Subcommittee to Investigate Juvenile Delinquency, Committee on the Judiciary, United States Senate (Washington, D.C.: Government Printing Office, 1973).

14. Maturity–Myth or Reality?

How many of us have said, "Oh, they'll grow out of it!" "They're just kids!" "He's just going through that stage."? In such expressions, we are suggesting that people will get there, given time. But where is it that we are going? Our answer, almost like the next stop on a flight from New York to Los Angeles, would probably be, "To maturity, of course."

Maturity is a vague concept that suggests we have made it and now are supposed to be adults and, therefore, responsible. The idea of maturity is important for families to grasp because it is not only our goal in raising our children, but also our own goal in behaving as adults. What is maturity? And how does one get there?

In an article in *Psychology Today*, a team of Harvard researchers concluded: "The best we parents can do to help is to love them, and not stand in the way of their grasping attempts to grow up, or force them at all times to conform to adult-centered codes of moral behavior."[1]

They found that the key to "making it to maturity" for a number of young people was not one particular method of child raising; rather, two factors emerged as significant in the lives of those most mature:

- Parents—particularly mothers—really loved their children.
- Parents appropriately controlled their children's expressive behavior.

It was found that children receiving both love and an appropriate measure of control were likely to achieve the highest levels of social and moral maturity. We will examine these two factors in greater detail later.

For now, let's look at maturity. What are its qualities? For the adolescent, it is captured in words like responsible, self-supportive, good self-image, able to cope with life's demands, able to make decisions that will have a positive effect on their own lives and others.

Psychologist Erik Erikson specifies four stages of *psychosocial development* that help to further define maturity.[2]

> **Stage I:** *Receptivity*—showing respect for authority or tradition. Emphasis is placed on behaving properly, obediently, and decently. Thus, one aspect of maturity is our behavior. Does it show an ability to obey and to respect the direction of others?
>
> **Stage II:** *Autonomy*—emphasizes self-reliance, and an ability to make decisions independently from others. Characteristics of this stage are willpower, determination, courage.
>
> **Stage III:** *Assertion*—characterized by doing well in school or on the job; developing skills; learning to appreciate music, nature, or art; speaking with confidence; get-

ting along with or influencing others. The presence of these qualities leads us to expect that a person is doing well in the aspects of life he or she is engaged in.

Stage IV: *Mutuality*—relates to an individual's ability to understand other points of view, serving others for the common good. Stage IV differs from Stage I (decent behavior) in that it demands that a person understand others, not just be obedient.

In summary, (1) *respect for authority*, (2) *ability to make up one's mind*, (3) *ability to do well in chosen areas*, and (4) *ability to understand and serve others* are all measures of how well we have achieved maturity. These are stages of psychosocial development, each building on the former, with Stage IV seen as the highest level of maturity.

Closely allied to Erikson's four stages are three stages of *moral maturity*[3] as suggested by Lawrence Kohlberg:

Stage I of moral development is conformity based on external pressure.

Stage II, the intermediate stage, incorporates the standards of external teachers in the individual's own choices.

Stage III, the highest level, represents moving beyond one's own behavior into some unselfish concerns for others.

Given this progression, we would expect that maturity could be observed in an individual as he or she begins to make decisions based less on conformity, based less on an appeal to the authority of others, and based to a greater degree on a concern for others.

In the *Psychology Today* article, David C. McClelland concludes, "How can parents do right by their children? If social and moral maturity is important they should: love them, enjoy them, want them around; they should not use their power to maintain a home that is only designed for the self-expression and pleasure of adults; and they should not regard their children as disturbances to be controlled at all costs."[4]

Parents can easily fall into the trap of settling for the lowest level of social and moral maturity (obedience based on external pressure) at the cost of later full development. They may place such a high value on obedience to authority, and conforming to present standards, that they produce adults who can only conform to the authority of others and are unable to make decisions on their own. These parents fail to realize that promoting real maturity may, in fact, lead to a decrease in a child's predictable behavior patterns. As the child moves beyond this early stage of "receptivity to external pressure," he or she consequently moves toward autonomy and self-assertion. If obedience has been well-taught and modeled, this progression will be accomplished, though it will not be without incident.

STAGES OF DEVELOPMENT

What does this information suggest to us as young people, parents, and families? For one thing, it sets our task clearly before us. We can actually set family goals for discipline, growth, and development using these stages of moral and social development as guidelines.

Stage I

If, as is suggested, obedience and constructive discipline are important foundation blocks of maturity—Stage I—parents can establish these as goals for their children and for themselves. The task for the parent is to make sure their children have healthy, constructive habits and patterns of living to conform to, and that any pressure they use to promote conformity is constructive and not destructive.

This first stage is supposed to lay the foundation for future stages of moral development. Parents who teach their children helpful social skills; who increase their children's knowledge of the world about them; and who do this in an atmosphere of love, acceptance, and fair discipline are preparing their children well for Stage II, that of helping their children incorporate the standards of teachers into their moral choices.

Children who are forced to conform through manipulation (bribery) or physical abuse (power) may find it increasingly difficult to incorporate any ideas from other authority, because of their mistrust of their parents. For example, Teri had been manipulated and physically abused by her parents. Now at age 9, she can't tell the difference between good and bad authority. To Teri, all authority is suspect, and she is entering adolescence with a need to question the right of anybody to tell her what to do. For her, the seeds of rebellion were sown early in life.

Jeff, on the other hand, was raised in a family who nurtured his growth. His parents were able to admit their own failures and accept the consequences for their behavior. Jeff felt love and acceptance, which gave him freedom to learn from his failures, too. He was also beginning to learn that there were people who wanted to use him for their personal benefit, as well as those who had his best interest in mind. He was learning to accept some advice while rejecting other advice, after carefully evaluating it. Because his parents demonstrated good authority, he was well prepared to move into Stage II and incorporate the values and standards of others into his personal decision making.

Stage II

Conforming to family behavior that helps a person deal effectively with life generates a confidence, a positive reinforcement, that frees a child to consider the standards of other authorities. This capacity needs to be exercised and developed. Choices need to be made, actions considered in light of their consequences, and decisions made that lead to the best action. No longer can we expect the child simply to conform or obey.

Teri found it difficult to perform well in school. Resentment welled up in her, along with feelings of rejection whenever she was advised or corrected by her teachers. She neglected her homework and purposefully failed tests just to show her teacher that she could do what *she* wanted to do. Teri was not about to take anyone's advice; in fact, she often would do just the opposite.

Jeff found it easier to evaluate and adopt ideas from others. He had learned that good authorities could provide information that would help him make better choices.

Stage III

If an individual has learned to make good choices, he or she is well prepared for Stage III, an unselfish concern for others. This is regarded as the highest level of moral reasoning. Most mental-health professionals see the need for each of us to live in relationship to others. Thus, a selfish, or totally self-oriented, person is seen as immature and unfulfilled.

Teri had not learned to respect or trust the views of others. The consistent rejection and abuse she had experienced developed in her the tendency to immediately mistrust and reject the views of others. "They" were wrong, and she was not about to listen to "their" opinions or try to understand "their" points of view.

Jeff was able to see that others had views well worth listening to and trying to understand. Often his new understanding motivated him to "move in" to help others in need.

Though each stage of moral development lays the groundwork for future stages, we can become stuck in any one stage and fail to move on to the next.

GETTING STUCK ALONG THE WAY

Why do so many people live their entire life in conformity to other's expectations? External pressure can lead business people to sacrifice important areas of growth for success. They drive themselves relentlessly, doing almost anything to conform to the demands of others. Young people go against their parents, they subject their bodies to the devastating consequences of drug or sexual abuse, or they give up what they deeply desire for short-term acceptance and approval.

Pressure is a familiar concept in our society, appearing in such phrases as: "I can't stand the pressure"; "I can hardly wait 'til it's over"; "I've got to get out from under it"; "I *have* to get away"; "Don't push me"; "Get off my back." All of these imply that we are a society of victims who have not learned to cope with pressure. For whatever reason, it seems to me that there are a lot of children, young people, and adults who are operating at a Stage I level of moral reasoning. We are a society unable to cope well with requests to do things we really do not want to do and are not fit for us, but which we are being "pressured"—bribed—to do. A move to St. Louis with the company may be hard on the family; but, if you take it, you will be in line for a good promotion. Or we may only accept people who smoke dope, or who go to the symphony, or who dress like we do. Or we see people as Christians only if they speak in tongues or go to a specific church or are in a Bible study.

We are a culture vulnerable to pressure. Why? Because we don't know how to handle it. At times, we seem to be a directionless people, pushed and driven by something other than personal goals. External pressures, which are always there, but which should have lost their power to control us at about 8 years of age, continue to exert control over us long after we are adults. They reduce us to puppets controlled by our desires.

Many in our society have reached a Stage II level of moral growth but have not moved on to Stage III. These individuals are able to make good choices for themselves but are not able to tune into others. They do not understand the point of view that others express, and their own living habits tend to center around themselves. Though they are able to think for themselves, they tend to superimpose their own standards on others, rather than making an effort to understand what others need and then act on that understanding. This is particularly devastating in a family where the parents are stuck at Stage II. They make their children extensions of their own growth, rather than understanding that each child has his or her own unique needs.

For the Christian, these three levels of moral development toward maturity might be likened to the rich young ruler (Mark 10)—Stage I; the prodigal son (Luke 15)—Stage II; and Jesus's ministry—Stage III.

The rich young ruler felt the pressure of being controlled by external goods. He was rich and therefore found himself in a moral dilemma when Jesus challenged him for his own good (Stage II) to give his riches to the poor and come follow him. The pressure of external forces (Stage I) was greater than the new standards of the teacher (Stage II). He chose to keep the riches, lowered his head, and walked away.

The prodigal son, Scripture says, "came to his senses" and returned home—Stage II. It might be argued that the influence of his father, or other authorities around him, was incorporated into his choice to return to his family. It was a free choice, nevertheless, and possibly one he would not have made had he not opened himself up to the advice of those he respected. He did, however, come to his senses and decide to return to his waiting father.

The ministry of Jesus was, throughout the gospels, a servant ministry (Stage III), underlined with an unselfish concern for others. His entire purpose in living was to die a sacrifice that all might live. We are further advised that this sense of servanthood is the core of the Christian witness—"Just as I have loved you, you must love one another. This is how all men will know that you are my disciples, because you have such love one for another" (John 13:35, Phillips).

Though maturity, measured by social or by moral development, is not our chief end, it does give us some helpful and clear suggestions—suggestions that appear to be complementary to the biblical stages of growth to maturity mentioned in Romans and James. The primary goal of the family (Deuteronomy 6) is to establish a firm relationship between each member of the family and God. The developmental stages give us as parents additional help in planning for the healthy development of each family member.

REACHING THE HIGHEST STAGE

Only as an individual moves into the highest stage of psychosocial development will he or she be able to display the highest stage of moral behavior. Jesus makes a distinction between these stages of development time and time again when he shows that true goodness comes from the heart, not from blind obedience to a set of rules, even religious rules. He notes the importance of *receptivity* (Ephesians 6:1–3); *autonomy* (Mark 10:21,22); *assertion* (2 Timothy 2:15); and most of all *mutuality* (Romans 12:9–10). Jesus emphasizes that maturity is not an end in itself; it is the result of a person's openness to growth and development in the Spirit.

Tightly woven into God's plan for our lives are (1) responsibility of the parents (Proverbs 22:6); (2) tradition of the family (Deuteronomy 6); (3) dynamics of a healthy family atmosphere (Ephesians 4:6); and (4) responsibility of the greater Christian community (Acts 2:44–47). Along with these interconnected relationships is the lively, always ready, all-embracing movement of the Spirit of God. He is the crowning resource for the Christian family. It is the Spirit of God who ultimately aids and enables each parent, each adolescent, each child to achieve the maturity we all seek.

NOTES

1. David C. McClelland, Carol A. Constantian, David Regalado, and Carolyn Stone, "Making It to Maturity," *Psychology Today*, June, 1978, p. 42.
2. Ibid., p. 45.
3. Ibid. p. 50.
4. Ibid., p. 53.

Epilogue

There is no doubt in my mind about the importance of the family in the life of any adolescent. Despite evidence in our day that the family is gasping for breath, this God-ordained institution remains our most relevant setting for positive growth and development during this stage of life; it must not be converted into a mere hotel-restaurant-laundry facility as children reach their teens. It is clear to me also that families come in many different shapes and sizes, each capable of being both nurturing and destructive to its members. It is the responsibility of each family, as well as the responsibility of the church, to take seriously the task of "peoplemaking." This involves helping each other spot and evaluate the tendencies to be nurturing or troubling and to make changes where needed. It is obvious that many American families are falling apart. They need prompt revitalization for their salient role in shaping the future. Today there is no greater urgency for this revitalization than in families with pre- and early adolescents.

For those of us who have adolescents in the family, it is time to evaluate before God our priorities and to reestablish *family* high on our list. Then we must make effective plans to ensure that this priority is actualized. Our society's overemphasis on material possessions, dual careers, successful promotions, a prestigious social calendar, travel, etc. has subtly coaxed many parents to see their adolescents as interfering with their own personal fulfillment.

Let's remember that though most adolescents are almost grown, they continue to need a high level of involvement from their parents, along with a sense that their family will keep on as a family, even though roles continue to change. Deep in our spiritual roots—our creation—is a tug reminding us that God has given us a very special privilege and a mandate to develop and maintain a healthy family, no matter what form it takes.

Index